I0236548

My Life

Immigrant and Clinical Psychologist

By

John Martin Pinschof

Grosvenor House
Publishing Limited

All rights reserved
Copyright © John Martin Pinschof, 2022

The right of John Martin Pinschof to be identified as the author of this work has been asserted in accordance with Section 78 of the Copyright, Designs and Patents Act 1988

The book cover is copyright to John Martin Pinschof

This book is published by
Grosvenor House Publishing Ltd
Link House
140 The Broadway, Tolworth, Surrey, KT6 7HT.
www.grosvenorhousepublishing.co.uk

This book is sold subject to the conditions that it shall not, by way of trade or otherwise, be lent, resold, hired out or otherwise circulated without the author's or publisher's prior consent in any form of binding or cover other than that in which it is published and without a similar condition including this condition being imposed on the subsequent purchaser.

A CIP record for this book
is available from the British Library

ISBN 978-1-83975-818-8

Author and Margaret 2003

To:
My wife, Margaret

My daughters and their husbands:
Madeleine and Christopher
Elisabeth and Marcus

My grandchildren:
Annabelle and William
Samuel and Rosa

Foreword

This is a life story that begins with a fascinating, improbable, and occasionally funny family history, before focussing on the adventures of the author himself.

John Pinschof's early years were defined by the tumultuous events that overtook Europe in the mid-twentieth century. His family's journey from Austria to England, via internment on the Isle of Man, encapsulates the experiences that many young people of his generation found shaping and influencing them throughout the rest of their lives.

Settling in England, and experiencing some of the nuances and snobberies of its education system whilst living through personal tragedy, coming within seconds of a very unpleasant meeting with a German V-2 rocket, and having another brush with death whilst climbing in the Alps, helped shape an individual whose story is warm, humorous, and enlightening.

Marcus Primhak

Preface

I began to write this book as a personal record, and at the request of my family who have only ever heard snippets of my background and early years as the child of immigrants from Pre-War Austria and of the many very difficult years that followed, including incarceration in the Isle of Man, separation from my father for most of the war years and then his early death. I describe two episodes of near instant death, one during the war from a V-2 rocket and the other being a few feet from annihilation from falling rocks in the Alps. An eventful period of National Service followed eventually by University and qualification as a Clinical Psychologist and happy marriage.

I describe being the very first psychologist to be appointed to one of the UK's largest Psychiatric Hospitals and creating what I believe was the largest Psychology Department in the NHS within just a few years but amidst tension, opposition and eventual departure. There followed new appointments, including being appointed by the Secretary of State for Health to the new Mental Health Act Commission and, following retirement from the NHS establishing work in the Private Sector, which included a thriving practice for the Civil, Criminal and Family Courts. This led to representing the British Psychological Society in the Royal Courts of Justice Family Justice Experts Sub-Committee. Following a proposal from myself and a colleague, this led to The Family Justice Committee funding an investigation of all psychology reports that had been submitted three Family Courts over the previous three years. This resulted in a highly critical report and created huge controversy among affronted psychologists. The more recent cuts to Legal Aid led a group of psychologists to suggest a bizarre response, which I describe and which I believe I was part instrumental in quashing, saving the profession huge embarrassment.

I describe my anger at the "Brexit" vote but this led to establishing Dual Nationality for my daughters and grandchildren. A happy outcome. I retired after 50 years of a fulfilled and at times very controversial professional life into happy retirement and enjoyment of family life and four grandchildren.

John Pinschof

Contents

A letter to my grandchildren

The following is my account of my early life as an immigrant from Vienna and later in an eventful and sometimes controversial 50 years' career as a Clinical Psychologist.

It would be best for you to read it in conjunction with my mother's memoirs, which will provide you with many details of our early family lives. There is also a history of my great-great-grandfather, written by my grandfather's eldest brother. My sister Maria has also written about her memories of her life, including aspects of the family before and after the war. Her memory is probably more accurate than mine of those early years during the war, and should be read in conjunction with my account. We both differ in some of our memories, but there is no point in attempting to reconcile them both. My Aunt Florette has also written of some of her memories, but this is in German.

In separate files, you will find many details of the various branches of the family of both my parents. I have photocopied selected family trees I have in my possession, and you will get some idea of your heritage from studying these.

The Pirquet side is documented in much greater detail than the Pinschof side. I have prepared a very brief synopsis, which you will also find in a separate folder. But before you read any of them, I want to add some comments, or perhaps a plea.

Over the years, and especially when I have been in Austria in contact with relatives, some – though not all – have left me disturbed by what I characterise as 'hero worship' of some of our ancestors. Hero worship can be a problem when it implies the belief that the achievements of our ancestors are transformed into self-glorification.

What I want to convey is this: the achievements of our ancestors are their own achievements. They belong to no-one other than themselves. Their respective parents can possibly claim credit for providing good genes, but children, grandchildren, cousins, and all those who come after, are themselves – and only themselves. We can all respect and be proud of what our ancestors accomplished, but that is where it should end. Individual achievements, such as those of Clemens and Guido Pirquet, lead to fewer problems, as their achievements are very individual to themselves.

The more pervasive problem arises out of the many family aristocratic titles. Just because some ancestor was honoured (in the very distant past, and usually as a result of success on the battlefield) and the titles passed on through the generations, this has led many descendants to believe that they are equally grand. But no. You are responsible for your own achievements. That is as it should be, and the job of parents is to foster your ambitions and abilities. Your ambitions and abilities are yours.

Incidentally, Austrian titles were abolished in 1918. So, you will not see any titles, other than the German equivalent of Mr, Mrs, and Miss, in telephone directories or other official lists!

CHAPTER 1

In the beginning

I was the third child, my parents having had two girls prior to my arrival. The eldest Anna was born on 15th May, 1934, and Maria on 2nd April, 1936. Then I arrived on 16th September, 1937. Those familiar with those early dates will of course know that the 2nd World War started in 1939. This event changed completely the lives of so many millions of Europeans, including my family, who left Austria for the UK.

Few inhabitants of Vienna or elsewhere would have been able to predict the outbreak of war until it happened, so the Viennese living in the 1920s and 1930s would have been blissfully unaware of the horrors to come. Except, of course, for the Jewish population. I comment later on this period in relation to the Jewish population, but it was not pleasant. Strong anti- Semitism was very apparent and rife in Vienna in the inter-war years, but mostly hidden from the non-Jewish population; or possibly, a more accurate description is to say that the non-Jewish population preferred to turn their backs and pretend that nothing was happening. I do not know what exactly my parents knew or understood, as this was a topic they never spoke about. But they were certainly aware of the problem from 1938. As the anti-Semitism of the times became more out in the open, my parents certainly felt the pressure, and they were all too well aware of distant, and not-so-distant, Jewish ancestry in a number of lines, though they themselves nor their respective parents were Jewish. What I did come across from one strong Catholic relative in the 1980s, though I have forgotten who (it could have been a number), was the still common attitude prevailing at the time – and possibly still now – that anti-Semitism was quite understandable and even justified because 'the Jews crucified Jesus'. I think I was so shocked when I heard this comment that I have blanked out just who actually said it.

Whatever the above meant for my parents, it is evident from what I have learned is that they had a supremely happy life from the time of their wedding until the year when war broke out. It had been a genuine love-match – one, however, that caused my mother's parents considerable concern, presumably because of minor (to them major) differences of background. They sent my mother to Berlin to their cousins, the Mendelsohn family, in the hope that she would forget, but after a year in Berlin her parents gave up, on the advice of their cousin. So she returned and married at the age of 18 to the man she had fallen for over a year previously.

A characteristic of her family background was that far more emphasis was put into boys' education, with girls' studies being of lesser importance. Thus, though my mother married early, she was not brought up to learn skills other than housekeeping and domestic skills. This became relevant later on after the death of her husband.

My parents had built their own house in the village of Bisamberg, which was effectively a suburb of Vienna, about 15 miles to the north of the city. I am not sure of the date they moved in. They had previously been living in an apartment in the Stadion Gasse, no.2, one block behind the Parliament buildings.

I would like to be able to say that I was born either in this apartment or at the Bisamberg house, but I was born in a Viennese maternity ward. I have been told that I was a happy and confident baby before the outbreak of war, but not surprisingly I have no memories of this period and none at all until around 1941 in a very different country.

Obviously, I know nothing of this period in the run-up to the 2nd W.W. first-hand, and little of the precise details of this period in my parents' life, as they rarely spoke about it. This silence was typical of most people who lived through this period. I had to drag out memories from relatives who had stayed behind and who I spoke to many years later.

This period was, of course, dominated by the 'Anschluss', which refers to the German annexation of Austria on 12th March, 1938.

This was Hitler's attempt, deliberately or not, to correct the omission of Austria from the unification of Germany in 1871 – a move dominated by the Prussian-dominated Germany.

Whether or not my parents had been aware of the anti-Semitic atmosphere that had taken hold in Austria throughout the 1930s, I do not know. But a museum of that time of Jewish repression in Vienna opened only a few years ago, and it is clear that this period of Austria's history makes for extremely uncomfortable reading. What appears to emerge from this period, and from talking to the museum staff when we visited about four years ago, is that many Austrians and Viennese were, or pretended to be, unaware of what was going on beneath the surface. My parents seemed to have lived a comfortable life, eventually building their own house, while my father was working for Cook's/Wagon Lits.

Apart from historical reports, the earliest accounts of the German Anschluss have come to me only briefly from my mother and my sister, Anna. At the time, my parents had an apartment at No. 2 Stadion Gasse, situated just behind the Parliament buildings. This meant that the only comfortable place for her to take my two sisters and myself for a walk was to the nearby park, which just happened to be across the Ring Strasse and directly opposite the Parliament buildings.

Both my mother and sister Anna can recall the actual German Annexation of Austria, with the German Army marching into Vienna along the Ring Strasse – the road that circles the inner city, and runs past the Viennese City Administration building and Austrian National Parliament building. I presume it was a coincidence that my mother, Anna, Maria, and myself were in the park opposite the Parliament buildings just at the wrong time when the German Army marched in. I cannot imagine my mother taking us there if she had known what was about to occur.

Many years later, Anna recalled her memories of the Anschluss. Her most vivid recollection appears to be seeing armed soldiers perched in the trees along this road. Whether this is an accurate memory or not, I cannot say. I have never seen any photos of soldiers perched in trees, but I have seen photos of the German troops marching along the Ring Strasse. Maybe she did see them in the trees, or perhaps the entire event would have been sufficiently traumatic for a 5/6-year-old to feed her imagination. What is certain is that the pavements and the park alongside the street were crowded with Viennese people all shouting, 'Heil Hitler', and executing the Nazi salute. I have recently read that Hitler spoke from the balcony of the Heldenplatz, which is situated just to one side of the park where we had been on our walk!

My mother never said if she stayed in the park to listen to Hitler speak. It is very unlikely, though, even if she had known he was there. What she did do, or rather did not do, is what so many other Viennese citizens were doing, namely cheering and giving the Nazi salute. She refused to do so, which was noticed by the police, who took her name and address. She has said that she just wanted to get away from the area, but she could not get home as it meant crossing the Ring Strasse, which was full of soldiers. Instead, she was sure she could take refuge in the house of a cousin she was very fond of, and who lived with her father nearby. My mother walked away from the cheering crowds, but when she arrived, her cousin's father was on his balcony doing the Nazi salute! She never told me what she did then.

Police saw her on a second occasion, with my sisters and me in the same park, when German troops arrived marching along the Ring Strasse. Once again, the Viennese were all enthusiastically giving the Nazi salute and shouting 'Heil Hitler'. But again, my mother would not salute or join in, which was noticed, and her name and address taken by the police for a second time.

Alongside these two incidents, my father had been informed that he was to lose his job as Finance Director with Cook's/Wagon Lits, as it was to be given to a Nazi supporter. Therefore, with distant Jewish ancestry on all sides, and their all-round hostility to what was happening, my nervous parents realised that they could be very vulnerable. According to my mother, Cooks/Wagon Lits headquarters in the UK were aware of the problems and invited my father to England to discuss his position. She said they offered him the Finance Directorship in Paris. He stayed in England, but I do not know if he delayed going to Paris before taking up the post, or never intended to take the position. However, the war intervened, so he remained in England for us to follow. This was surely a very lucky break for all of us – the first of quite a few 'what ifs'.

Having decided to leave the country, my parents sold their Bisamberg house to their cousin, Lotte Leitmeier. The house itself survived the bombing, and I was able to visit her in 1954 and see the home my parents had been so proud of.

Back to 1939. Six months after my father had gone to England, and three weeks before the outbreak of war, my mother, Anna, Maria, and myself left Vienna to join him there. I have never known just why it had taken so long for us to follow. And we nearly did not make it.

My mother's account of the day we actually left Vienna was that we were taken to the train by the chauffeur/driver hired by, or employed by, our grandfather. I have also been told that we may have travelled by horse and cart. Either way, my mother recalls that the man was driving terribly slowly, as she believed he possibly did not want us to leave. The outcome was that we arrived at Vienna's Westbahnhof (West Station) just as the train was about to leave. My father's brother Karl was waiting for us, extremely agitated. As soon as we arrived, we were bundled onto the train, with our luggage put on elsewhere, because the train was already moving. It turned out that our train was the very last one to leave Vienna for the Channel ports before the outbreak of war. The second 'what if'.

I think we arrived first at Boulogne, and then Dover. (For another possible explanation of why we almost missed the train, see my later comments about when we first went back to Austria in 1949.)

My mother's memoirs recall that when we arrived at Dover docks, a huge crowd was waiting, but I am said to have almost immediately spotted my father before anyone else and yelled out, 'Papa'. No-one else had spotted him. He came aboard to help with the luggage, but first picked me up, and I apparently went instantly to sleep on his shoulder. Needless to say, I have no recollection of this incident.

We then took the train to London, where I understand that my mother's sister, Florette, met us. We were then to go to Chalford in Gloucestershire, to my father's cousin Carmen, but my parents were a bit nervous of arriving with three children, as they feared it might be too much for Carmen. So Anna and Maria went off in a taxi with my mother and Florette and I were put into a taxi with Molly Orley, who they had known in Hirschstetten, where she was either a guest or helper – I am not sure which.

Florette often told me that when the two taxis went their separate ways – she with my mother; Anna and Maria and me with Molly Orley – I screamed so loudly that she could hear me for a long while. In my mother's diary, she recalls that Florette accompanied me along with Molly Orley. If so, I can understand that she heard my screams. It certainly appears that I did not take too well to this separation, coming as it did so soon after seeing my father for the first time in many months. I apparently ate very little for the next three weeks, and am told that about the only thing I did all day was walk around the house holding a cat by its tail and swinging it behind my back. To put an end to my obvious misery, my parents collected me after three weeks.

When you all read this, I feel it would wrong and certainly not fair to be too harsh in your judgment of my parents for leaving me behind. It may appear rather odd, insensitive, and perhaps unfeeling, if not cruel. However, given the circumstances, they would surely have become far more traumatised by their situation than any of us these days can imagine. They would surely also have understood that Carmen and her husband would have also been nervous about the upcoming unknown turmoil.

Maria says that this experience damaged me, as I became nervous whenever any stranger arrived at the door. And perhaps it did. I do have one memory of running to my mother and clutching her skirt and hiding behind it, just peeping out to see who was at the door, but I have no idea just when this was. Be assured, I do not do this now! But did this decision, plus the early separation from my father, do lasting damage? Again, I do not know – nor does anyone know what the alternative of no war and all that came with it would have done for me. All I know is that we were all immeasurably better off than millions whose fate was unthinkable. So I have no criticisms or complaints. If I was damaged, it was for all the right reasons.

Maternal Grandparents: Johanna & Silverio v. Pirquet

Paternal Grandmother: her children:
top L: Eva. Bottom Left: my father. right; Karl

Pirquet family home

Authors Mother

Authors Father

CHAPTER 2

England, Chalford, the Isle of Man, return

My father's cousin Carmen, and her husband Arthur, loomed large in our lives in varying ways until their deaths in 1955/6. They lived in Chalford, Nr. Stroud, Gloucestershire. Carmen was one of three daughters of our paternal grandfather's brother, who had immigrated to Melbourne, Australia, with his wife – a noted singer and then singing teacher. Born in Australia, Carmen married Arthur Harris, an English businessman. All I ever knew of his business life was that he had been a representative/salesman for Nestle, and had spent a lot of time abroad in Vladivostok, Russia. I do not know much more than that, but he must have made a pile of money as he and Carmen lived in a large 18th Century Georgian house with huge gardens, orchard, and woods. It sold for £3000 in 1955/6, after their deaths, but would now be valued in the many millions.

I had always presumed we lived with them for a while, but my father had obtained a job with a neighbouring farmer who raised and trained foxhounds, so we then lived in a cottage belong to this farmer. Until recently, when my sister Maria corrected me, I had always thought this cottage belonged to Carmen and Arthur, because I recall it as having been situated at the end of a long, back drive in their grounds. My first, and very indistinct, memory after arriving in England was of my mother cleaning and dusting that cottage.

I am not sure how long we lived in Chalford, but I know from endless tales that we were soon sent to the Isle of Man. This was where the government sent the many thousands of refugees from Europe, because they believed that there were bound to be some Nazi supporters and/or spies among them, pretending to be refugees. Therefore, the safest thing for the government to do was to send them all to the Island. I doubt if it prevented genuine spies from attempting to operate in the UK.

The irony was that we were not technically refugees, as my father had come to England about six months before the outbreak of war. We were technically 'migrants', so should not have been sent to the Isle of Man. However, it appears that my mother's sister, Florette, who was training to be a nurse in Stroud, was sure we were sent there because of Carmen's husband Arthur. She always believed he had reported us to the police to protect his reputation in the vicinity and among his Freemason fraternity. We will never know, but whatever the reason, off we went.

The decision to send us to the Island left my parents with a difficult choice. My sister Anna had already started school in Stroud, so they had to decide whether or not they should leave her with our aunt in Chalford or take her to the Isle of Man, with no certainty that she would get into any local school. They decided to leave her in Chalford to continue her schooling in Stroud, living there as a weekly boarder and staying with our aunt over the weekends. Was this the best choice for Anna? We will never know.

Having arrived in the Isle of Man, we were put up in a large house overlooking the bay in the small port of Port St Mary, on the southwest corner of the island. This is the first house I can recall. My mother's sister, Florette, was also sent to the Isle of Man, and I presume she travelled with us, but I do not recall ever hearing her talk of this period in her life.

I have very few memories of that year's stay. What few memories I do have are of being given a teddy bear and giving it a haircut, and Florette admiring my hair-cutting skills!

Another memory was seeing my mother swim out to sea in the bay, and I saw her clearly hurting herself as she stumbled while wading back, damaging or breaking a toe. She recalls this incident in her own memoirs as having damaged her toe as she swam out, and she continued to feel this injury for the rest of her life whenever the weather turned cold.

A very vivid memory, which is as clear now as it ever was, is of two identical nightmares. They consisted of a hole appearing in the ceiling directly above my head, and then seeing a snake slowly sliding through until it was just a few feet above me – at which point I woke up. I never mentioned this to anyone at the time or since, until now! I have no idea why not. Nor did I analyse this dream, then or since, which I am sure Sigmund Freud would have done, no doubt with interesting speculation.

I can also recall seeing many convoys of ships passing the bay. I cannot be sure if they were leaving (what would have been Liverpool) or returning. Probably both, as I have a dim recollection of seeing ships in very irregular patterns, while on other occasions I seem to remember they appeared to be far more orderly. Presumably the irregular patterns were of the remaining returning ships that had survived the journey unscathed by German torpedoes. On another occasion, I can recall a German fighter plane floating in the bay, with its pilot still in the seat, bobbing back and forth along with the plane. By the next morning, it had gone.

An extraordinary and very odd experience occurred around 2005/6 or so. The BBC broadcast a series of programmes in conjunction with the Open University, called Coast. This series explored the UK coastline and eventually got round to the Isle of Man, mentioning – among other topics – its role in housing refugees during the war. Margaret was watching the programme and came rushing up to say the programme showed a photograph of two rows of women, and she felt sure one of them was my mother. My memory is that I also saw this programme and the photo, and was sure I had spotted both my mother and Florette! I now have a copy of this photo, but unfortunately it is not clear enough to reproduce here.

I rang the BBC producer, who put me in touch with the Isle of Man Archivist. She knew of the photo and broadcast, having provided the information for the BBC programme. She said she would send me a copy of the photo, but told me later that she deliberately did not mention that the photo depicted two children sitting on the floor at the front of the group. She said she wanted us to get a surprise if they turned out to be my sister Maria and me. When the photo arrived, it duly depicted two children sitting on the floor in front of the group – and they were indeed Maria and me! My mother was in the photo, in the back row, but there was no Florette. This photo is the only memento of our stay on the Isle of Man.

As you may read in my mother's memoirs, while she and my father were on the Isle of Man, she had no idea exactly where my father was on the island. No contact had been allowed between any wives and husbands. I just cannot imagine how stressful this would have been for both of them, and I also cannot really understand the thinking behind this policy. Just what secret German or Austrian spies posing as refugees on the Isle of Man could get up by way of sabotage, spying, or general insurrection, is difficult to understand. I can only presume it was a reflection of the general rational or irrational hysteria, and fear of what might happen next in the fight against Germany.

The men were, in fact, encamped behind barbed wire somewhere on the island, probably around the capital, Douglas. My sister Maria said my father was incarcerated in Douglas Prison, but I am not sure if there had been one or more camps.

As we discovered, and were told later, the refugees turned the camps into an intellectual hot house. Among them were musicians, three of whom later formed the Amadeus Quartet – arguably the most famous quartet in the UK in following years, and who went on playing well into the early1980s (the 4th member of the quartet, the cellist, who was not a refugee, was the last to die around April/May 2020). I had not known of their history on the Isle of Man until many years later, and certainly long after both Margaret and I saw them performing at the Free Trade Hall in Manchester.

One man my father had become very friendly with was a fellow Austrian, who after the war became a Benedictine monk in Prinknage Abbey in Gloucestershire. My father later became an 'Oblate' in this order, which is a kind of lay, or associate, or half monk! I recall him taking me to visit and staying overnight. I had a room (a cell) to myself, and I remember finding the horsehair mattress the most comfortable mattress I had ever slept on! Maybe that does not say much for the other mattresses I had been accustomed to.

My mother told me many years ago, described also in her own memoirs, of another 'what if'. While on the Isle of Man, we had been told that we were to be sent to Australia. This apparently led to panic, as they were not sure if Anna was to go as well or what would happen to her, and led to frantic telephoning and writing to and fro. However, eventually we were not sent, but I had always believed that the ship we would have been put on was torpedoed and sank with total loss of life, which would of course have included us. My mother's memoirs recall that the ship that would have taken us was in fact sunk on the previous trip to Australia with the first contingent of refugees, with a total loss of life.

Of interest is another sinking. I have seen a reference to another German torpedo attack sinking a ship on its way to Canada, also full of refugees, drowning most of them. (See entry below when I write about the John Fisher School and the famous athletic coach, Franz Stampfl, who was on this ship and survived a 10-hour ordeal in the sea.)

After one year, we returned to England together, with a letter of apology from the Home Office, but I have very few memories of this period.

From later accounts, I know that my mother then obtained a job as housekeeper and cook for two families, and she had very fond memories of one family, a Mr and Mrs Lacy, who lived in East Hendred, Oxfordshire. I have just two memories of this period with Mr and Mrs Lacy. One painful memory is when I saw a small bright red 'sweet' lying on the floor in front of a coal fire. I picked it up, but it was definitely not a sweet! I recall screaming and my mother plunged my hand into a tin of flour, which I recall offered some respite. On another occasion, I remember finding an Army helmet, putting it on, and playing on a very steep slope next to the road. I slipped and fell head first onto the road, but the helmet saved me from further damage. On reflection, I suspect that this sleep slope was no more than about one or two feet high!

During the period after our return from the Isle of Man until we arrived in Woldingham, Surrey, I cannot recall ever seeing my father, even though my mother's account of this period in East Hendred mentions that he was living nearby, wherever he could find work. So I presume I must have seen him, and in fact on many occasions.

We then moved to Woldingham, Surrey, where my mother had found a job as gardener and/or housekeeper for a lady living on her own. We were provided with a cottage next door, Red Roof Cottage, where we lived from approximately 1943 to 1945. The cottage was situated next to a very large golf course.

My father had obtained a job as a cashier at the Dorchester Hotel, London. I have always believed this was obtained with the help of my mother's sister, Annamirl and husband Peter Bally, whose parents were hoteliers in Switzerland and who also owned the Browns Hotel in London. I cannot be sure if this memory is accurate or not, though, as I have never thought to ask my cousins.

My father was able to visit us every so often, and although I don't have many memories of his visits, I do have some. My parents were very devout Catholics, so we all had to go to church on Sundays, with the nearest being in the town of Oxted, situated at the bottom of the steep slopes of the South Downs. This involved walking down a steep road and past a chalk quarry (still just visible from the M25). This was easily do-able on the way down, but hellishly steep on the way up, and exhausting after a long church service and no breakfast. Once, on the walk back, I recall getting a lift on my father's back, which I loved, and of which I still have a very clear memory – particularly of his sweating body!

Another less enjoyable memory (except in retrospect) is of being in that church for Sunday mass with just my mother, sitting about halfway down on the right side of the church. Midway through the service, I suddenly produced a huge belch! This panicked my mother, who immediately took me out. But instead of just leaving our seats and immediately walking to the back of the church, she took me down to the front of the right side, then walked across the entire front, past the altar, to the far side, and then to the back of the church and out! I remember this church sightseeing tour causing me much more embarrassment than the belch.

Another vivid memory from this time was of me exploding at my parents when my mother referred to me as 'Hans'. This was, of course, what I had always been called, being the diminutive of Johann in German. And I had been called Hans throughout this early period in England and the Isle of Man. But from around the age of five, while living in Woldingham, I apparently insisted on being called John. I can imagine that this must have been quite a difficult command for my parents to follow.

I have a very distinct memory of all of us sitting down to a meal with both parents, and my mother again calling me Hans. I exploded, screaming at her and insisting that she call me John! Neither my mother nor father ever called me Hans again. I recall thinking at the time that Hans was just a silly and ugly word, but I suspect that deep down I hated it because I had somehow understood its connection with Austria/Germany. Maria tells me that I had insisted that the school we attended in Caterham should also call me John. And I have been John ever since.

On another occasion during breakfast, I remember a more pleasant incident. Having finished eating a boiled egg before my father came to the table, I turned the egg upside down on his eggcup and howled with laughter as he tried to open it. He pretended not to know! Eggs were severely rationed during the war, but we had our own supply, as our parents had managed to buy six chickens which we kept in the garden. Anna, Maria, and I had our own pet chickens – mine being the smallest, and which I called Tiny.

I have no memory of the food, except for eggs, which for the general population was a luxury. I think the official weekly ration for each individual was one egg per week. What I do recall is the regular rosehip syrup provided free for each family, plus free cod liver oil (disgusting) and malt, a very nice thick black syrup. In addition to these food items, we were all provided with a gas mask. Perhaps a gas mask was more vital than a deep shelter, which was not available in the heart of the countryside. Instead of the latter, we had to make use of the cupboard underneath the stairs, and I do have memories of being in this 'shelter' on a few occasions. It is just as well its strength and safety were never put to the test.

If readers look up the location of Woldingham on a map, you will see that it lies on a path towards the East Kent coast, thus being in a direct line from southern England airfields to Germany. Therefore, it was also in the direct line of the V2 rockets – or doodlebugs, as they were called – coming the other way, and from enemy fighter and bomber planes, of which thankfully there were few at that stage in the war. I can recall seeing just a few 'dogfights' between German planes and our Spitfires and Hurricanes.

From 1944/5, it seemed that the whole of Surrey, Kent, and Sussex was covered with barrage balloons. One was situated about 50 yards down the road in the front garden of a house. They were supposed to catch the V2 rockets in the wire that held the balloons, and I presume they had some success. Our house was near the southern edge of the North Downs, and when we walked to the edge we could see much of Kent and Surrey. When the balloons were flying, all you could see was a horizon filled with literally hundreds of these barrage balloons, all flown at different heights. It was an amazing sight.

In spite of our location, I do not recall ever being in a vulnerable position or of being frightened, with just two exceptions. This was partly quite realistic, as this part of Surrey was not an obvious target – the main ones being about 15 miles or so to the west. But two particular memories do stand out from this period.

The first memory was when our father, Anna, Maria, and I had been walking across the golf course situated just to the side of our house, when we heard a doodlebug (V2 rocket) fly over. We heard its engine stop, which indicated it had run out of fuel. We followed the instruction we had been given through public warnings over the radio, which was to immediately throw ourselves to the ground, lie flat, and count to seven. And just on our count of seven, the doodlebug exploded as it hit the ground! We certainly felt the force of the explosion, but were unhurt. When we got home, we saw our mother covered in white dust! She had run to the one corner of the house where the ceiling had collapsed, and which landed on top of her! But she was thankfully unhurt.

Another occasion was far more serious and, but for a breath of wind, the house, my mother, Maria, and I would all have been obliterated. I was in the garden with Maria on a beautiful summer day when we heard the approaching sound of a doodlebug. It had not yet run out of fuel, but was flying very low. We looked up and saw it flying in a very shallow descent, and heading directly for our house, garden, and us. Suddenly we both panicked and threw ourselves behind a hedge (all of two feet high!), fearing we would be hit within a few seconds. But then, what must have been a breath of wind saw it slowly veering to its left, and we heard a crash a few seconds later. We saw in the newspaper headlines the next day that it had landed about one or two miles away, killing two cows. I suppose the moral is 'never complain of the wind', but it was another one of many 'what ifs'.

There are other memories of this time. Apart from frequent sirens, all giving warning of enemy aircraft or doodlebugs on the way, the summer of 1944 was characterized by beautiful weather in the evenings. We were in the direct line of flight of wave after wave of British and US bombers travelling overhead on their way to decimate German cities. This was the so-called 'carpet bombing' of German cities, perhaps the most controversial aspect of Britain's conduct during the war. What none of us could have known was that in the last few weeks of the war one of these bombers would drop a bomb through the centre of our grandfather's house in Hirschstetten, a suburb south-east of Vienna. I describe later of seeing another consequence of this bombing in Cologne.

Anna had re-joined us some time in 1944. She had continued to live with our aunt in Chalford when we returned from the Isle of Man, so that she could continue her schooling. When she returned to live with us, I can recall going to the local train station to meet her. She got out of the train, and I remember her being sullen, stern, and giving not one indication that she was pleased to see us. She had been five years old when we'd arrived in England, and separated from us for around three years. So she was old enough to have felt that separation. Maria recalls her describing the time when she was left with our aunt while we went to the Isle of Man. Apparently she said she cried and cried for two whole days, but then decided she just had to get on with her life and make the most of it.

But back to Woldingham. In the last summer of the war, there were still many bombing raids on London. When these occurred in the evening, we could see the entire horizon to the west of us lit up by the resulting fires. This area would have been South London and Croydon. It would have been a beautiful sight, were it not for the awful destruction it caused. Anna would always rush upstairs to look, as I did a few times. Our mother always tried to stop us, insisting we stayed in the cupboard under the stairs, with our gas masks ready to hand!

At some point, Maria and I started attending school, which was run by nuns in Caterham, and involved us travelling there on our own by bus. I have very few memories of this school, but I presume I must have learned something. I do remember having to lay our heads on the desk for a few minutes in the morning and try or pretend to go to sleep. I can also recall (once only) having a peeing contest in the outside toilets, to see who could reach the furthest! Another memory, which I have never ever mentioned to anyone, was when I desperately needed the toilet (bowel evacuation) while on the bus going home from school. As I stood up to get off the bus, the action of standing up led to me being unable to hold out. Someone must have had the unenviable task of clearing up a perfectly formed turd, left behind on the seat. Moral: do things as soon as they need doing!

As the war ended, my mother obtained a job in a Catholic school run by nuns in Lechlade, Gloucestershire, namely the Convent of St. Clotilde. This job came with accommodation for us all, but not for my father. Accompanied by our six chickens, we went by train from Woldingham to Victoria Station, then to Paddington Station to catch the train to Oxford. We then changed again to get the train to Lechlade, where we were met by the convent's horse-drawn cart, which took us, our luggage, and our six chickens.

We were given rooms within the convent, and were well looked after. Sometime after we arrived, the entire school went by coach to nearby Cirencester to wave flags for a ride-past by the

King and Queen, as part of their tour of Britain in celebration of the end of the war. I missed it, as I had a serious bout of whooping cough and was confined to bed for a few weeks.

The school was primarily a girls' boarding school, and for most of the time I was just one of two boys in my class. I have few other memories of this place other than competing with this one other boy to see who would finish bottom of the class in the end-of-term marks. I think we took it in turns. Again, I have no memories of our father visiting us during what must have been about a year's stay, but I am sure he must have done.

Being a convent as well as a school, the nuns seemed to spend an inordinate amount of time in the chapel. They had a resident priest, and it was taken for granted that I should be taught to serve and be an altar-boy at mass and all other services. I do not recall ever having been asked if I consented, but it continued in Purley and at school later when I was a boarder. Perhaps this was a lesson in 'obedience'.

CHAPTER 3

Purley, Surrey, and first return to Austria

In 1946, our father obtained a teaching post at the John Fisher School in Purley, Surrey. We then bought a house at 32 Purley Park Road, which was situated below a high embankment, on top of which ran the electrified Southern Railway trains. This was a source of endless curiosity as the trains went past, especially the Brighton Belle. Before long, I knew the names of each carriage painted on the sides. Even more exciting was the occasional steam engine train.

This house cost the grand total of around £300! It was a lot of money for us, but was still comparatively cheap even in those days, as it still had some war damage, mainly with some ceilings having collapsed. It took time to get all the damage repaired, and the problem was that the winter of 1946/7 was one of the coldest (until matched by the winter of 1962/3), with deep snow lasting for weeks. After some of the coldest nights, it was impossible to see out of the windows in the morning as they were all iced up. We had hot water bottles in a largely failed attempt to keep us warm before we went to sleep. But this meant putting our feet on top of the water bottle and not moving, as every other inch of sheet was freezing.

The water pipes often froze, except for the pipe in the upstairs toilet. It still had an old gaslight which we kept on all night, thus stopping the tank from freezing, so we could at least have a semi-decent sit-down in the morning, often with the help of the newspaper to do the necessary! We survived.

The school playing fields were covered with deep snow for weeks during that winter, and on a few occasions one of the priests used his motorcycle to tow pupils and staff around the field on skis. My father took the opportunity and did well, not falling once.

A continual source of excitement for me, as well as the passing trains, was watching the road from the upstairs bedroom. The interest was a house nearly opposite from which two taxis operated. When I heard them leaving or returning, I had to rush to the window to watch. This may seem inexplicable today, but there were hardly any cars on the road in those days, and still fewer which drove on our street. Some lorries, such as refuse lorries, were the most frequent other vehicles, while most other delivery vehicles were horse-drawn. Whenever a horse vehicle passed, my father used to run after it to pick up the inevitable manure to spread on the garden!

It was during the three years we lived there that my parents visited second-hand furniture stores in South Croydon and bought the ornate chest of drawers that we now have in our sitting room, as well as the clock on the mantelpiece and two 'utility' armchairs that are still in use in the guest sitting room at Minster Abbey. Utility furniture was a special hard-wearing but cheap-to-make range of furniture designed during the war. These stores were full of incredibly cheap household furniture and other items, presumably salvaged from bomb-damaged or destroyed homes.

Some very strong memories of this period concern our food. It was clear to us that there was not much money, so there were many occasions when we came home after school and our tea consisted of slices of bread and dripping, alternated with bread and sugar. We had no problem in devouring as much as we could, but it was an odd contrast to the three individual silver mugs – each of us had been given as a baptismal gift – now used as our drinking mugs. Two other food memories are of our mother cooking the most delicious roast mutton. I can still taste it. We also had frequent fried herring, also delicious. I presume these items had been very cheap buys at the time.

A consequence of the sparse, though good, food was that nothing was ever left on my plate – and that is still the case. It is also why some in my family may have noticed my irritation when just about everyone invariably leaves behind some food, even if only scraps.

I went to the John Fisher School where my father taught, while Anna and Maria went to St Anne's – a Catholic school run by nuns. The John Fisher School was a private Catholic school, founded by the Archbishop of Southwark. It was in essence what would later be called a comprehensive school, catering for all boys, but it then started a 'grammar stream' as a result of the Government's educational reforms outlined during the war by R.A.B. Butler. The emphasis was on the importance of providing a Catholic education, but this led to what in retrospect would prove to be a major handicap. The headmaster, Canon Byrne, and most of the teachers were priests who had been to Oxbridge, mostly in fact to Cambridge University. Therefore, on the presumption that they must have some brains, the Archbishop assigned them to a teaching role! No doubt this was done in all good faith, but looking back I feel it was a mistake! They were all well intentioned, but were poor teachers. Teaching was not why they had become priests.

I do not have that many memories of the first three years at this school, other than either walking all the way, or later cycling to school with my father and back on my own. This meant cycling along main roads for what must have been one or two miles each way. It would be unthinkable now for a seven- to nine-year-old, but at that time there was very little traffic, even on the main roads. An additional hazard for cyclists in those days was the trams, and getting to school and back meant crossing the tramlines. Many accidents occurred when the bicycle wheels got trapped in the tramlines, but with my expert cycling (!) I managed to avoid such a fate.

School itself was always a bit of a trial, as anyone who has ever had a parent teaching in the same school will know. However, a much greater problem, which haunted me every single day, was having to endure the morning roll call. The issue was my surname – and we were all called by our surname. There was the obvious problem of other boys calling me 'pinch-off', but worse was that, to me at least, it was clearly very different to the average English name. There was only one other foreign name, that of another Austrian boy with the surname of Bertelle. I always felt at the time that my surname sounded weird, but looking back it is clear that the real problem was my own association of the name with Austria/Germany and all that that implied. To this day, I still have a residual embarrassment at the name, which is why I was so pleased – in fact, very moved – when both my daughters, Madeleine and Lissie, clearly felt otherwise. They have very proudly given all four children the name of Pinschof placed before their surname.

When I was eight or nine years old, I went down with mumps during one term, measles during the next term, and then scarlet fever in the summer term, leading me to miss most of that school year. Scarlet fever was at that time thought to be a dangerous and contagious disease, and meant one had to go to an isolation hospital. Although I had been ill for about three weeks while the GP pondered on the diagnosis, I was beginning to feel much better by the time he decided what was wrong with me. This meant he had no option but to arrange for me to be sent away to be incarcerated at an Isolation Hospital for three weeks, and of course visitors were not allowed. I remember my mother peering through a window and waving at me, maybe once or twice, but she was not allowed onto the ward.

I have very few other memories of those weeks. The strongest and most enduring memory was of what was happening to the boy in the bed next to me. I never knew what his problem was, but it involved being given two injections every 24 hours, both into his stomach. The day nurse regularly produced howls and screams of pain, but the night nurse was able to inject him without so much as a whimper. (That gave me an early lesson in psychology.) Years later, in 1987/8, I visited this hospital as a member of the Mental Health Act Commission (see below), and I recall seeing the exact block I was incarcerated in, and the actual window my mother would have looked in. It had later been converted into a mental hospital and looked it, but was empty when I saw it, ready to be demolished.

On another occasion in 1947/8, I made the big mistake of telling my parents that cycling for a few minutes up a slight slope left me short of breath! I presume my parents feared I had a heart problem, as they immediately contacted our GP who arranged an appointment at London's Guy's Hospital. My father took me. We got there almost first in the queue, but waited for about two hours. Eventually, my father complained, and the secretary apologised, saying she had mislaid the notes!

When it eventually came to my turn, I was examined by what I presumed was a junior doctor and, having been made to strip and given a gown to put on, I was ushered into a large room with banked rows of seats, occupied by dozens of junior male and female doctors, with 'God' sitting in grandeur in the middle of the floor: The Professor! I was told to take off my gown and had to stand there naked in front of everyone while 'God' talked about and above me. Horrible. The arrogance. 'God' was God, though, and patients were his exhibits. But what were they looking at? My heart was not visible; nobody has a heart visible from the outside.

I had a reminder of this experience In 1996/7, when I saw a client for therapy and, in passing, she referred to her son having had an appointment at Guy's Paediatric Department. She expressed outrage at her son having experienced exactly the same indignity as I had. Clearly the culture and the sheer arrogance had not changed; it was worse than outrageous. He could not have been the same 'God', but perhaps he was the Son of God.

We had few visitors at Purley Park Road, but I recall my mother's brothers, Hubert and Peter, visiting. When Hubert came, I noticed he was wearing what I felt was a beautiful wristwatch, and I could not stop ogling it (to my later embarrassment). After a while, he took it off and gave it to me! I wore it from then until about 1970/71, when Margaret gave me the Heuer watch for my birthday that I still wear. I also recall a visit by another friend of my parents from Vienna. He was a cellist in the Vienna Philharmonic Orchestra, which was in the UK where they played in the very first Edinburgh International Festival. I was most impressed.

I do not have that many other memories of these years. One is of my father spending his evenings studying. He had not been to university in Vienna, so now he had enrolled in what I had always thought was Trinity College, Dublin – or London University, as my sister Maria recalls – for an external degree. On one or two occasions, when I was late going to bed, I remember seeing a table in the sitting room covered in books and writing pads. He was teaching the subjects he was learning at the same time, which I think were Latin and Greek. If I am vague, it will be because I was more often than not in bed by the time he started studying.

Some vivid school memories include the food. While I was still a day-boy, we had endless puddings of tapioca and sago, both indistinguishable, which we called 'frogspawn'. Both were ok but fairly tasteless. I believe this was a standard ration for all schools during the late 1940s, in the days of food rationing. But before we proceeded to the puddings, a lot of the boys used to leave their food, especially the meat. Whenever I noticed, I asked them to pass me their plate and I ate whatever they left. I recall thinking that I wanted the meat because I just liked it, but looking back I presume it reflected the fact that I was often starved.

In 1946, my brother Toni arrived on the scene. My mother told me he had been conceived to celebrate the end of the war! He spent a lot of the time in his pram out in the garden to get fresh air. When he cried, which he often did, he received little attention. Crying was apparently OK! My mother would often say crying was good for babies as it exercised their lungs. She implied that this was the common prevailing view, by which I assume she meant amongst her family. However outdated it appears, it is almost certain that this came from her own childhood memories of her mother, who was said to have been a very poor mother. However, leaving babies in the garden and letting them cry was also the 'zeitgeist' then, stemming from Trudy King – a famous paediatrician of the time who also advised on regular regimes and many other long discarded truisms.

My brother Toni was doted on by us all, except by me in the odd moments when he would get hold of my toys and throw them about. He once threw my favourite toy, a model ambulance, down the toilet. It had been a present from the Bally family, my mother's youngest sister's family.

Anna, Maria, and I used to get weekly pocket money of three pence and then later six pence. Enough to buy an ice cream on the way back from school or, if we saved up for a few weeks, enough for a cinema ticket for Saturday morning showings. Another memory is of a big battle over me wearing some new boots I had been sent from the U.S.A. by the Hochfilzer's. I hated them, as I knew of no other boys who wore boots, but after a huge argument and tears, I lost the battle.

Everything changed in our lives from 1949. One morning when we got up, our mother told us to be very quiet and to get our own breakfast, as our father was in bed with a massive headache, and any noise was intolerable. We went to school as normal, but got back home to find he had been taken to the local Mayday Hospital in Croydon. He was there for about one week. Children were not allowed to visit anyone in hospital! No doubt another edict ordained by another God.

Our father was diagnosed with a brain tumour, so was then transferred to the Atkinson Morley Neurosurgery Department in London, now part of St George's Hospital in Tooting, South London. We were allowed to see him when he was being put into the ambulance for the journey. When he was in the ambulance, we three – Anna, Maria and I – climbed in to say goodbye. He looked at us and told us how much he loved us. This comment went through me like a bolt of lightning. We then bent down to kiss him goodbye, stepped out of the ambulance, and that was the last time we ever saw him. About two weeks later, he died. My mother came home after we had all got back from school and told us that he had died, and promptly collapsed into an unstoppable fit of crying.

Making the comment he did about loving us was the first and last time any parent, relative, or any other adult had ever said such a thing. It was simply not the kind of comment parents made to their children in those days – at least, not Austrian parents, or perhaps just parents from my family. It seems it was just not in their culture.

Maria has reminded me that after my father died, our mother asked the two of us to walk to the parish church, about one mile away, to tell the parish priest what had happened. Maria recalls that she did all the talking, but I have no memory of this.

The next painful episode was at school. Either the day after he died or the following day, we had our usual music lesson, and the teacher, Mr McHugo, began to rehearse what I immediately recognised as 'Mass for the Dead'. I put my hand up and asked, 'Why are we doing this?' The whole class froze. I could hear the silence. The poor man was speechless. I instantly realised why, and wished the floor would swallow me up.

When it came to the funeral, I did not travel to the church with the family, but had to get to the church earlier as I had to serve as an alter boy. I dared not look at my mother or the others in the front row in case they were crying, as I was afraid I might then start. I cannot remember if I had volunteered to serve, or if it was simply taken for granted, because I had always been an altar boy at this church (every Sunday Mass and often afternoon Benediction service). The burial was at Bandon Hill Cemetery, Wallington, Sutton (near South Croydon). When it came to throwing holy water and earth into the grave, my memory is of my mother being on the point of collapse and would probably have fallen into the open grave if Florette and Annamirl (her sisters) had not grabbed her and held her up. I believe I just blotted out this trauma for much of my life since, and have always found it difficult, if not impossible, to talk abut.

A few months later, after Toni had stayed with my mother's sister Annamirl and her family for a few weeks to give my mother some respite, my mother read out a letter she had received from Annamirl's three children – our cousins Peter, Silvia, and Claus. They suggested that, to make things easier for our mother, we should send Toni to them, and they would look after him and bring him up. All three of us (Anna, Maria, and I) instantly screamed 'no'. We were all incredibly angry at the suggestion that, having lost his father, Toni should now be taken away from the rest of his family. I am sure they meant well, and looking back it was clearly a very generous and heartfelt offer. What our cousins' parents thought, I have no idea, but I can only presume they had agreed to the idea. We will, of course, never know the outcome for Toni if that suggestion had been carried out.

However, we carried on with our lives. We had a visit from my father's elder sister Eva and her husband Hans Hochfilzer at some point after my father's death, but I do not recall just when it was. I do not remember them coming to England at any other time. I would imagine that the contrast between the UK, living on rations, and the U.S.A. at that time would have been too great to have enjoyed the experience. But on that occasion, they took us to the Dorchester Hotel for lunch. I knew enough about the hotel scene in London to know it was one of the poshest hotels in town, particularly favoured by wealthy Americans. While I cannot remember the menu and what we ordered, I do recall thinking at the time that the lunch was nothing special and was very disappointing. Having said that, I am not sure just what I had expected, as we had never had any experience of any other hotel at that time as a point of comparison. It may well have been that some of the meals I can remember my mother having cooked were far better.

They then took us in a taxi to Cheltenham to stay for a night at a very posh hotel – I think the Queen's Hotel, again one of the grandest in the West Country. But this time I cannot recall if the food was any good, or anything else about the trip.

Throughout our stay in Purley, I remember food parcels arriving regularly from the Hochfilzer's. The only food item I recall was Spam, which arrived in every parcel, but my memory is that it tasted much better than the Spam we get in our supermarkets nowadays.

After the death of our father, we sold our house and our mother was offered her old job back in Lechlade with the Convent of St. Clotilde, together with accommodation for all of us. I was to go back to the John Fisher School, but as a boarder this time. Out of a school of around 350 boys, there were approximately 50 boarders. The headmaster had agreed for me to stay for free until I left school – clearly a very generous gesture, as my mother would have been incapable of affording the fees. Anna and Maria were taught at St. Clotilde, which was also a private school, and I presume the fees were incorporated into whatever salary my mother was given, which would not have been much. Anna later went to Studley Horticultural College in Warwickshire, and in her last year Maria went to Rye St Anthony School in Oxford, then St Andrew's University to read Psychology.

Life slowly settled down for the remainder of that school year. But over the summer of 1949, before I started school as a boarder, my mother took us to Austria for the summer holidays. She had wanted to see her father, who she had not seen since she left Vienna.

If readers recall my account above of how we nearly missed the train when leaving Vienna, here is another possible explanation instead of, or in addition to, my mother's explanation for our late arrival at the Vienna Station. We were still living in Purley, and were to travel to Austria by train. The rail station was about a comfortable 15-minute walk from our house, but our mother spent the last half hour before the train was due to leave tidying up and dusting, while we were going frantic. She would not stop. We were sure we would miss the train from Purley to London Victoria Station, which meant we might miss the train from London to Dover, and would then miss the boat from Dover to Ostend, and then miss the train from Ostend to Austria.

With about five minutes to go, we were all screaming at our mother to leave the dusting, which she then did, leaving us to run with a heavy suitcase to the station. We arrived late, but the train was also late leaving the station, so was still there. A very relieved family managed to catch it, but this episode has always left me wandering just why we almost missed the train that left Vienna all those years before. My mother's behaviour on that day was not an aberration. It was typical! This may also be why I always insist on leaving home for any appointment, etc., in plenty of time! (I do not recall ever having missed any bus, rail, boat, cinema, theatre etc.)!

Anyway, we caught all the connections, and took the train from Ostend to Ebensee, Austria via Cologne. The train had surprisingly extremely comfortable wooden slatted seats, unthinkable these days, though I can imagine that adults might not have been so comfortable. We had a four-hour delay at Cologne before the train set off again, so my mother took the opportunity to get off the train and see Cologne, noted for its large and beautiful medieval Gothic Cathedral. Maria and Anna refused to come with us, being terrified that something was bound to go wrong, so they stayed on the train.

We walked through the station, which to my surprise looked newly-built, but I did not understand the significance of this until we exited the station. To the left was the huge Gothic Cathedral, looking vey sorry for itself, streaked as it was all over with black (with hindsight, black burn marks or soot?).

I then looked to the rest of the city, and there was nothing there! Apart from a few buildings immediately in front of, and behind, the cathedral, not a single building throughout the city was left standing. You could see for miles in all directions as far as the horizon, the city being fairly flat, and every building had gone – empty – a whole city had disappeared.

How many air raids it took to demolish Cologne, I do not know, but what was clear was that it would have taken wave after wave of bombing from the British and American bombers to have flattened the city – the very bombers that had flown over us in Woldingham evening after evening. No doubt the train station had also been demolished, but had been the first building to be rebuilt. I think the reason for my surprise at this level of destruction was that by then we had heard such a lot about the bombing of such cities as Dresden and Hamburg, but rarely had there been any mention of Cologne.

When we got back to the train, I don't recall any mention being made of what we had seen, but we found Anna and Maria both very upset, as the train had moved to another platform while we were gone, and they had thought it was leaving for Austria without us! Apparently, it had taken a considerable amount of reassurance from other passengers that the train was just changing platforms!

We eventually arrived at Rindbach. The rail route went along the west side of the large Traunsee, with mountains along the opposite bank, including the 5546.48 ft. Traunstein. I recall being initially wholly underwhelmed by the scenery, as I think I had imagined that the mountains would somehow have appeared twice as high as they did!

We eventually arrived at our grandfather's house, but found it was all rather strange. For example, the toilet did not have a 'U' bend, and flushed outside to a pit in the garden! Yes, it smelled!

After a day or so we got used to the smell, and it just disappeared. But I do recall being extremely uncomfortable for the first day or two.

Our grandmother was still alive, but died the following year, so this one occasion was the only time we saw her. She had suffered some brain injury when she fell off her bicycle during the war, but this was not at all obvious, even when we had been informed.

A painful memory of that first visit was the many German lessons my mother had arranged for us, taught by an elderly local witch.

In retrospect, what was strange was that for the entire six weeks we were there, no-one mentioned the war or anything that had happened in the vicinity. I found out only years later that there had been a concentration camp nearby – the Ebensee camp (Ebensee being the nearby town).

We experienced the local thunderstorms, which are to be heard to be believed. With the thunderclaps being trapped inside the ring of mountains, the thunder was magnified to an extent we had never heard in our comparatively flat topography in much of England.

Our grandfather taught us the Austrian card game Tarok which was enormous fun. Some years ago, when Margaret and I were in Edinburgh, we found the game on sale so bought it with the intention of teaching Madeleine and Lissie how to play, but we never have got round to it. Sorry.

Our mother took us back to Rindbach for the next two summer holidays, but Anna never came with us again. In 1951, my mother's sister Florette and Franzl got married, and I persuaded my mother that I wanted to be there for the wedding, so I left early and went back on my own. Florette insisted that during the reception I drank too much and became extremely 'happy', or so it was alleged.

There was a major trauma, which I only heard later after my mother and Maria got back home. I had gone from Rindbach to Ebensee rail station, only to discover that I had left my passport behind. So my mother cycled back to Rindbach and back again with the passport, just in time for me to catch the train. The effort must have been immense, and in fact too much. What I discovered later was that she then walked to the Ebensee Church, and apparently when she got there might have had a heart attack, presumably caused by her over-exertion in getting my passport. She was not taken to hospital, though, as she fairly quickly recovered.

During one of these holidays, my mother bought a carved crucifix from a local sculptor, Hans Kienesberger, who I understand later acquired a national reputation. I thought I would love to have a crucifix as well and a statue, promising I would pay my mother back later. Of course I never did! I still have them, as they are lovely carvings.

For all of these three holidays in Austria, we saw a lot of another of my mother's sisters, namely Annamirl and her three children. They also used to holiday in the area, but in a house on the Grundlsee, a lake about 20/30 miles away. They would often visit our grandfather and us in Rindbach. A real treat for me was when we all piled into their car – a beautiful right-hand drive, British-built, soft top Daimler, with a boot that opened to expose two extra seats. I have never seen another model like it.

My memory of which of our three holidays we did certain things is rather hazy, but in either our second or third visit we all climbed the local landmark mountain, the Traunstein. We went with an uncle and his wife and young daughter Barbara, who would have been around eight or nine years old. I will always remember her, as she was clearly very impressed by me! She kept looking at me with wide eyes, in total admiration!

We returned to visit our grandfather for the next two summer holidays, but were no longer subjected to German lessons from the witch. On our second or third holiday, or both, I remember our grandfather commenting that he did not want to be buried together with his wife in Ebensee, because he did not want to be eaten up by the same worms that had previously feasted on her!

I must have returned from that visit with an odd collection of coins, as I have recently re-discovered in my possession a small collection of foreign notes. Three Italian notes for 5 lire each, one for 10 lire, and another with what could be a portrait of Mussolini on it (a 50-lire note). I have no idea where they came from. There are also two 20 Frank Belgium notes and one 50 Frank French note, plus a 50 Groschen Austrian note, with the following printed across the top of one side: ALLIERTE MILITARBEHORDE. What the word Militar is doing there is perplexing. Could it be a note from the time of the German Occupation? How did I acquire them? I have no idea.

My father, 1948
(the single photo of my father taken from the larger family group)

CHAPTER 4

From boarding School to National Service

After that summer holiday, I returned to school, but this time as a boarder. I mentioned earlier that the headmaster of the John Fisher School had very generously allowed me to attend as a boarder for free until I left school. However, my mother received an itemised bill from the school Bursar before the start of term, and I had the embarrassment of having to go to him to tell him my mother had been promised free boarding and schooling for my entire stay at the school. He never made the same mistake again.

We had heard that two years prior to my becoming a boarder the then boarding master, another priest, had been sacked for getting involved in some scandal. He had clearly been a very effective boarding master from some aspects, as he started a tradition whereby the 50 boarders (out of over 350 pupils) had invariably held down a large proportion of places in the various school sports, such as cricket and football. We never found out what variety of scandal/abuse he had perpetrated, but assumed it had to do with boys! He was sent packing, but was given a job as a parish priest in some diocese in Sussex.

On one occasion fairly soon after I started as a boarder, I was called to see the Headmaster, Canon Byrne. Without any preliminary comment, he told me my father had confided in him that he had wanted me to become a priest! I remember being taken aback and said nothing, then walked out of the room. Such a career choice had never entered my mind, before then or after.

I went back to Lechlade during all my holidays, sometimes by train, which involved going from Paddington to Oxford and then getting the branch line to Lechlade, which was closed later in the

Beeching cuts. Both trains were pulled by steam engines, and though the noise was more interesting than modern trains, my memory of steam engines is very different from the current romantic view of them. Arriving at one's destination was always accompanied by shirt collars being turned black with soot at the edge. However clean the inside of the train, there was always some soot in one corner or another. At other times, I went by coach, which were both cleaner and direct to Lechlade. I can only presume that all those elderly characters so nostalgic about steam trains have either never travelled in one, or did not mind, or perhaps did not notice, getting dirty and grubby.

Another priest took charge of the boarders, and he was extremely good if rather strict. He not only kept order, but also maintained the tradition of having the 50 or so boarders holding around half the places in all the school team sports. But he left after two years (after my first year as a boarder) to be replaced by another priest. Though the new one was very pleasant and approachable, he was unable to keep discipline and the morale of the place slowly collapsed, to the extent that the fabric and play equipment became more and more damaged, and involvement in school sports teams dropped to almost nil. He left to become a monk in Aylesford, Kent, some years after I left. From what I understand, while the school is still a private Catholic school, the headmaster and most of the teachers are no longer priests but fully qualified teachers.

While the school was pleasant enough, it cannot be said to have been a leader in academic excellence, though I am ready to believe it was better than some. With respect to its small boarding contingent, it is likely to have been light years in advance of the feudal practices one hears about at such major public schools such as Eton, where senior boys are allowed their own 'fags', otherwise known as younger boys who must obey their elders, i.e. senior boys. The sense of entitlement that bestows on the senior boys can be seen throughout the ranks of the Conservative members of parliament.

The school policy, or rather the Catholic Diocese policy, of teacher recruitment from Oxbridge did leave its mark. I can remember when a boy one year above me obtained a place at the University of Reading to study geography. The reaction of one of the priests was 'what, Reading?' No doubt he would have made the same comment if he had heard I had also obtained a place at Reading University many years later. Shocking! All the priests had been to a Cambridge or Oxford Catholic college!

I did not particularly distinguish myself during my years there, but did pass all my exams at '0' and 'A' levels with one exception which I describe later. But in one area I did succeed. When I entered the 6th form, I was made a Prefect and given the job of looking after the youngest class every morning. Until then, this class had the reputation of being rowdy and difficult to control. I walked into the class on my first day and, sure enough, they were making an almighty noise. I just stood quite still and slowly turned to look at each boy in turn, and magically they all went quiet. And I never had any problem from then on! A psychological triumph! Was this a foretaste of the future? Probably not!

While the school was not noted as being a beacon of educational standards, it did have one example of excellence. One of the more inspired priests (in athletics, not teaching) arranged for an Austrian athletics coach, Franz Stampfl, to come and coach at our school. He had been to the Olympic Games in Berlin before the war, and been disgusted with the militarism that he saw there, so he decided to leave Austria and came to England. However, during the war he experienced wartime internment. One account I have read said he was put in prison, but I do not where this was. He had then been put on a boat – the *Arandora Star* – that was headed for Canada, but it was hit by a German submarine attack, and sank. Some 600 or so passengers were killed or drowned, but he managed to stay alive for about ten hours by clinging to a raft. He was then sent to Australia for internment, and by a weird coincidence, sailing on *The Dunera* – the same ship I travelled on some years later to Japan, during my National Service. After he returned to the UK, Franz started his athletic coaching career.

Franz Stampfl coached Chris Brasher, who then went on to win the Gold medal in the Steeplechase during the Melbourne Olympics, and became famous after having 'advised' (not coached)

Roger Bannister prior to him breaking the world record for running the mile in under four minutes for the first time. 'Advised' was the elitist term for coaching used by those athletes who were too grand to be merely coached!

At that time, every public school was a member of the Public Schools Association, which held an annual inter-school athletics competition. All the top public schools such as Eton and Harrow competed, and although John Fisher School had previously taken part, they had rarely achieved anything other than perhaps one or two boys gaining the odd third or fourth place. But in the first year after Franz Stanmpfl arrived, we won the entire competition with 18 points, which was a record! In the second year of his coaching, we won again with 24 points, and the third year we won with around 42 or 44 points!

The English Amateur Athletics Association (AAA,) under whose auspices the competition was run, was so incensed at our upstart school winning three years running that they withdrew the entire school championship and held it thereafter as a competition between individuals, with no accumulation of points for each school. This really was a pathetic and childish response from the elitist men of power of that era. If that was not enough, such was the way of the English at the time that the chief of the AAA, Harold Abrahams, who had been an UK Olympic athlete and Gold medallist, offered Franz Stampfl a coaching post with the AAA. The rumour that went round our school was that he would first have to join the Freemasons. He refused, and did not get a job within British athletics.

Soon after this rejection, Franz Stampfl went to Australia and coached many of their athletes, some of whom went on to success in the Olympics, winning many Gold medals. Franz Stampfl had one other unique claim to fame: he coached me in the hammer, and I managed to throw at least once over 100 feet when I was around the age of 14/15. (But it was with a lower weight of hammer – 4kg instead of 7.26kg. Well, one can always dream.)

This same priest who obtained the coaching services of Franz Stanmpfl might have been keen on athletics, but he was a lousy teacher. The custom in the school was that the senior master taught religion to the 5th ('O' level) form. He was the senior master, so readers can judge how good he was. Out of a class of 45 boys, only one passed, with the boy with the next highest score (me) having failed.

I became friendly with one day boy, David Kenyon, who lived just behind the school grounds. We had become friends when we discovered that we both liked classical music. One Saturday, we took off to see an opera at the Davis Hall in Croydon. I have no memory of what we saw, but I still have a huge regret that I did not accompany him to another performance – this time of a Wagner opera. In those days, I had not 'discovered' Wagner, and was feeling a bit sniffy about him, i.e. just prejudiced. Much later, I discovered that the Wagner performances at the Davis Hall were conducted by the generally considered world's greatest Wagner conductor of his day, namely Reginald Goodall.

This also reminds me of a film that was shown to us boarders of a famous pianist by the name of Paderewski, playing Chopin and Liszt. It made an enormous impression on me. The pianist had long flowing hair, as of course all really serious artists did, and he had also been the Prime Minister of Poland after the 1st World War.

It will be difficult for anyone under the age of 75 to 80 or thereabouts to remember the era of National Service, when all men from the age of 18 had to serve two years within the armed services. Us boarders received a cruel reminder of this National Service two years before I left school. One of the boarders, two years older than me, had left school to do his National Service, and was sent to Korea where he was blown up in a tank and killed. This was a year after fighting had stopped.

Another boarder left the following year, also to do his National Service, and was killed in Malaya, taking part in the long conflict that had commenced there between pro-independence fighters and the then British Commonwealth Territory in 1948, and only ended in 1960. He was drowned in a lake while undertaking some military exercise.

I have one memory of when I was in my last year at school that may have shaped my later decision as to my future career. I recall having visited my local library in Purley, which I did most

Saturdays, and borrowed three books – one each by Freud, Adler, and Jung. I have no recollection of the titles or the contents, apart from Adler writing about inferiority complexes, but I do recall being impressed and pretending to understand them. But I do not remember having really convinced myself even then that I understood much, if anything, of what they each had to say. I left John Fisher School in 1955, before heading off to do my two years National Service.

I cannot resist writing of just one other memory of my last year at school. This was of another sixth former coming back one day recounting a job interview he had been to, possibly for entering the Navy. He was asked what he would do if he was in London on the Strand and saw a Battleship coming towards him. He replied, 'I would torpedo it.' An astonished interviewer asked him where he would get the torpedo.? The boy said he replied, 'from the same place that you got your bloody Battleship' Naturally, the rest of us fell about in hysterics.

From our earliest days in England, our family spent many of our holidays in Chalford, Gloucestershire, with my father's cousin, Carmen and her husband. These ended when they both died a few months apart in 1955/6, just after I had been enrolled in the Army. We spent mostly summer holidays with them, but I also recall at least one Christmas holiday. I always looked forward to these holidays, not least because as soon as we arrived, I would always make a beeline for the dining room where they kept their old copies of the *Daily Telegraph*, the *London Illustrated News*, and the photo magazines, the *Illustrated* and the *Picture Post*, all of which I devoured from cover to cover. These have all long since ceased publication, except for the *Telegraph*. I used to think that the *Telegraph* published both the 'news' and its comment sections objectively; only later did I realise it was a heavily biased Tory newspaper.

Carmen and her husband's house was huge, and on one holiday we went into an unused room on the top floor which was basically as a storage room, and I discovered some drawers full of used postage stamps – many still with their envelopes – from destinations all over the globe. This is when I started stamp collecting, but more importantly, where I learned all my geography. It was also in this room where we laid out our model train, which we used to play with for hours. I have no idea where this train set ended up – just like my few Dinky toys that have vanished.

Carmen was a woman of habit, with a fixed routine for the day. After she got up, she used to prepare breakfast and then lunch. When this was all done, she had her daily bath, which had been filled by the housekeeper who came in the mornings and worked till after lunch. The only variation on this routine was when she went shopping in Stroud, always being taken by taxi. I used to accompany her whenever I could, and was always intrigued by the various cars that turned up. In Stroud, I accompanied her into the various shops, and was fascinated by one in particular, called I think 'International Stores', with its rows of open biscuit tins where you could order as many or as few biscuits as you wanted – a practice long since discarded.

There was never that much to do during the day, so one day I decided to dig one long garden bed full of irises. Somehow, I got through most of this until I put the fork through my foot, just above a toe. I still have the scar.

On another occasion, Carmen's sister Elisabeth and her husband had come over from Australia on a visit. A feature of this visit was that the two sisters were constantly arguing with each other during meals, to the extent that on one occasion the argument became so fierce that my mother fainted! The two combatants were mortified and apologised, and the arguments did become less fierce after that! On another occasion, Elisabeth's husband decided to do some very heavy pruning on a beautiful fuchsia bush, to Carmen's horror when she saw it. Another huge argument followed, and I felt Carmen was right –the bush had been desecrated. Then there was consternation, with Carmen in furious hysterics, over an incident when a stray dog appeared, no doubt on a casual visit to her own dog. They got up to things that dogs often get up to, but the last thing Carmen wanted was a litter of puppies.

Another fixed routine in this house was Arthur reading the *Telegraph* in his study in the morning, then he'd progress to the dining room just before lunch to have his daily dose of Gordon's 'Gin and It' –the IT, of course, being Angostura Bitters. From about the age of 14, I was invited along and he poured me some gin, but I always had it with lime juice! He often offered to fill up my glass, but even then, prudence stepped in, and I declined – or I think I did. I am not too sure. His afternoon usually found him in his study watching TV, and I often joined him. On one such day, suddenly and completely out of the blue, he told me that my father had been silly not to take up the offer from Cooks (his employer in Vienna) of a top job with Cooks/Wagon Lits in Paris. This was the first time I had known anything about this job offer. I did not know what to say, but even then I immediately realised that it was in fact a pretty good decision on his part, given the Nazi invasion of France and Paris very early on in the war. Had we gone there, our later lives would certainly have been very different – and possibly a lot shorter.

Another habit of Arthur's was to order a taxi every few weeks to take him to what Carmen called his girlfriend who lived on the opposite hill! About the only other event that I was aware of that led to Arthur getting out of the house for the day was when he went to his Freemasons' meetings. On one of these occasions, I can recall him being picked up by a very polished and dapper looking gentleman, who was introduced to me as having been the officer in charge of the company of the Gloucestershire Regiment when it had been involved in the famous battle of the Imjin River, also known as Solma-ri or Gloucester Hill, in Korea. I remember being most impressed, as I had been very familiar with this event, as we all were at school. This was a very famous battle during the Korean War, and had been plastered all over the newspapers at the time. They both then left to go to their Freemasons' meeting.

In the summer holidays of 1952, I went to Austria to stay with Karl and Susie, my father's brother and his wife. I still have the receipt for the train journey, bought at the Austrian Travel Agency, which was then in Shaftesbury Avenue, London. The trip was for a 3rd Class rail return via Ostend, Munich, and Salzburg, with a sleeper both ways, plus a permit for Vienna. The cost of the basic ticket was £18.13 shillings and 5 pence! Plus £3.3 shillings for the sleeper. The permit was needed because Vienna was situated in the eastern military zone of Austria, which was still under the control of the USSR Army, even though Vienna itself was under the control of all four powers – namely USA, UK, France, and USSR. This arrangement lasted from the end of the war until the Austrian Peace Treaty of 1955.

For the non-historians reading this, it took as long as it did for the four powers to sign the treaty, because the USSR did not want Austria to fall into Western European influence. It only agreed to sign a peace treaty after Austria undertook to remain neutral between the West and USSR. My Aunt Susie would often tell me that her father, who had been the senior civil servant in the Austrian Foreign Office, had been the senior negotiator that led to the peace treaty. Many years later, I think when Margaret and I were in Vienna on our honeymoon, or possibly later still, we saw an exhibition of photos in the Belvedere Palace in Vienna, with one photo showing the signing of the Peace Treaty, and Susie's father standing in the middle of the back row.

On my 1952 visit, I stayed with Karl and Susie in their Vienna apartment, but after a week or so we all went to Oed, a small village about 30/40 miles south-west of Vienna, and still within the Russian Zone of Occupation. This was the old summer retreat of the Pinschof/Herzfeld/Pichler family for years.

Karl and Susie and their then very young son, Thomas, lived in what I suppose had once been an apartment over some stables. It was very nice, too. There was another large house in the spacious grounds which was owned by our Pichler relatives, who always appeared rather aloof. But Karl took me one day to the old Pinschof/Herzfeld house nearby on the main road. It was totally empty, and looked as if it had been unoccupied for years. Quite a few objects were still around, including a very nice hairbrush, which I was allowed to take. Unfortunately, it disappeared at school – presumably another boy decided it was indeed very nice! I knew who it was, but had no proof. There was not that much to do in Oed, but we did go for walks in the mountains, the last eastern outpost of the Alps. One of the mountains we climbed, the Rax, was one of a close group of mountains that provided Vienna with its drinking water, and still gives the city its reputation for high quality water to this day.

Another memory that had interesting ramifications years later, concerned tennis. There was a tennis court in the grounds, and Susie would often play along with two male friends who travelled in from the nearby town. On many occasions I was invited to play and make up a group of four. Their standard was, needless to say, much better than mine, but they were very patient with my performance! Tennis highlighted a characteristic of Susie, which was that she, like all Viennese, was famous for her constant grumbling. The Viennese have a special word for it, namely 'raunzen'. She kept up this Viennese habit while playing tennis, always after missing a ball, over-hitting, or not being as mobile as she had been in her youth. She would constantly say she could no longer play as well as she had in her youth, when she claimed to have been very good. I presumed she was correct in her self-assessment, but was doubtful that she had been as good as she implied. Then on one occasion after she missed an easy shot, her 'raunzen' and her following boast became ever more outrageous. She said she had been so good as a young player that she had played in tournaments representing Austria! 'OK, right, of course you did. Tell me another,' was my reaction, although I managed to keep it to myself. Just.

Susie went on to tell me that she and Karl had visited his sister Eva and her husband Hans Hochfilzer in St Pauls', Minnesota, USA, for two years running in the mid-1930s. Susie said she had entered the USA North West Tennis Tournament, and on the second year she had reached the final! Of course she did. How could I possibly have failed to spot her old skill? But she then related that when it came to the final, the weather had been extremely hot, even by the standards of the USA Midwest. She claimed that her opponent had been regularly supplied with liquids, but that Karl never bothered to supply her, so she just lost all her energy – and so lost the final. I never believed a word! (I refer to this incident later.)

In the last week of this summer holiday, we all went back to Vienna to their apartment in Dannerberg Platz. They lived on the third floor of a very swish and typical Viennese apartment block, situated on the corner of the road, which looked onto a very large town square/gardens. (If the readers watch the film *The Third Man*, there is a scene when a man leans out of a window and a boy on the streets keeps shouting. The building depicted is exactly like Karl and Susie's apartment. The gardens must have been a lovely park before the 2nd World War, but unfortunately, the Nazi regime had built a huge concrete bunker in the middle of the square. It is one of four such bunkers, which are so massive and built to withstand any and every size of bomb, that they are far too expensive and almost impossible to demolish.

There were two highlights of my stay in that last week. Karl suggested I go to the Vienna opera. He gave me a ticket or a 'pass', explaining that the family had their own 'box' which they could use whenever they wanted. I suspect this had been Susie's family box, but never dared ask. Anyway, I enjoyed a performance, sitting on my own. The other highlight was visiting Louise Gerstner – a cousin of my father, and the wife of the owner of the very famous Viennese Konditorei 'Gerstner'. Her husband was still alive then, and I recall him inviting us for drinks in what was then the highest building in Vienna. I remember asking for Port! I was also invited into their Konditorei on the Karntner Strasse, and went down to the basement to be fed whenever I was in the vicinity – at their expense! Naturally, I took up this invitation as often as I could. There is a story that the Gerstners had provided the catering for my parents' wedding, but that the bill has never been paid. My grandfather would have been responsible for paying – or not.

Another holiday to the continent took place in the summer of 1955, when my sister Maria and I went on a hitchhiking trip to Austria and back. One lift we obtained was from a Belgian Army officer. He seemed to think we were trying to get to the nearest train station, so took us there. But he had to go to his own apartment first, and began to pour us both a large glass of neat gin. We could not think what to do with it, but when he left the room, we watered a pot plant.

When we got to Austria, our mother was already there, presumably having been in Rindbach, but an old family friend had offered us the use of a boat house for a week, situated in St. Gilgen on the Wolfgangsee. Maria and I joined her there, as did our Uncle Karl for a day's visit. Also ensconced in a very posh hotel about 50 yards higher up, were Hans and Eva Hochfilzer. One evening, we had to endure the most tremendous thunderstorm. When surrounded by mountains, as the Wolfgangsee is, the noise of thunder is hugely magnified. Suddenly a clap of thunder from almost overhead caused the most tremendous and sudden noise, making both Maria and I jump, but Maria jumped the highest – about two feet in the air! The next day we walked up to visit Hans and Eva, and saw a pine tree in the hotel grounds with clear, newly-made scorch/burn marks trailing down its trunk. A highlight of that week for me was being taken out on the lake in a sailing boat. The owner of the boat, who I had been told was or had been an international yachtsman, invited me out for a half hour sailing trip.

The holiday ended with Maria and I hiking back home via Switzerland, where we had arranged to stay with Annamirl and Peter Bally. I remember one extremely hot day in Tyrol, and while waiting for a lift I took my jacket off and put it over the fence just behind us. A lift duly arrived, and we piled in and set off. I am not sure how long it took us to realise that I had left my jacket on the fence with my passport in it. Panic! But it was too late to go back, so the next few days in Zurich were spent with Peter Bally very kindly taking me to the British Consulate and making the necessary arrangements for a temporary passport. This involved being taken by Peter to his place of work, where he was the company lawyer, and being taken up to the Managing Director of what was Peter's Chocolate. I was ushered into a large room with a huge desk in the middle, behind which sat an equally huge and expensively suited individual who, with a great flourish and even greater sized pen, signed a document to vouch for my identity. I was very grateful for all the help, but the few days were ruined because there was no time to do all the sightseeing our aunt had planned. I still have a letter from the Foreign Office to my mother, dated March 4, 1955. It reads:

'I am directed by Secretary Sir Anthony Eden to inform you that certain articles, thought to be the property of your son, together with a passport, have been found in Innsbruck and returned to the British Consulate. I am to enquire if you are able to confirm the loss of the property and, if so, to give some indication of the articles concerned. I am, Sir, Your obedient servant.'

After returning from this holiday, I still had a few weeks to fill before I had to make my way to the Hillsea, Portsmouth, barracks of the RAOC. Florette got in touch with Barbara Pirquet, the wife of my mother's elder brother Toni, who lived near Reading. Her four children were still at home, and I recall having a very pleasant few weeks with them. It was the first time I had encountered John, Caroline, Elizabeth, and Antoinette, who I still see from time to time, but not nearly enough as they and we have all had our own busy lives. During my stay, I became rather bored after a week, so cycled into Reading and went into the very first factory I passed and asked if they had a job. The answer was, 'When can you start?' I said, 'Now.'

So, I started the next day, and survived three weeks of excruciating boredom, operating machine tools that formed tin plate into biscuit tins. However, I discovered to my surprise that it was easy to make mistakes and turn out poorly stamped tins – not by me, but by the other operatives. Apparently, I made almost no errors, always turning out perfectly formed tins, and after a week the foreman put me onto another machine tool that was used to form their most expensive biscuit tins which were lined with the thinnest of gold plate. Presumably these were for the most expensive biscuits or chocolates made for 'Huntley and Palmers', who were situated in Reading. However good I had been in turning out perfect gold-plated tins, the job was so mind-blowingly dull that after three weeks I could not face another day, and handed in my notice.

Many years later, when returning on a visit to Reading University for a special rowing event, I met a member of the Palmer family. The family had donated millions of pounds and land to the university over the years, and were still very much involved with the affairs of the university, though their business had long been merged into another large chain.

CHAPTER 5

National Service

When it came my turn to leave school in 1955, I had to notify the relevant government department that dealt with National Service that I was eligible to be called up. I had not applied to go to university, which would have meant I was able to delay the call-up.

I was surprised, which is putting it mildly, to get a reply that I had dual nationality and could waive my eligibility to do National Service in the British Forces, but I would then be eligible for call-up in the Austrian Forces. It was only ten years since the end of the war, so the thought of ending up in the Austrian Army was simply not an option. It took me less than a second to reject this possibility. So I ended up in the British Army, being assigned to the Royal Army Ordnance Corps. I had fancied asking to join a Scottish Regiment, such as the Black Watch, because I thought I would look really good in the ceremonial uniform. Sense prevailed.

What surprised me was how many other recruits had never ventured outside their home town, especially those from the north. One in particular said he had never been out of Rochdale, and even within Rochdale he had rarely ventured further than his immediate area. For such men, or rather boys, National Service must have been an incredible experience.

After six weeks of basic training, which took place in Southsea, Portsmouth, we were then sent to the Corps Headquarters at the Deepcut Barracks in Surrey, near the main military headquarters in Aldershot. This was for four weeks of basic skills training, which meant learning about the work of the Corps, where Army warehouses were situated, and similar such issues. (Deepcut Barracks was involved in a series of odd and dreadful scandals in the last 20 years, with accusations of young recruits being bullied and some even killed). We were taught about the Ordnance Corps, as well as a whole load of basic personal skills and even given hygiene lessons. My only memory of these lessons was being taught to wash our hands after going to the toilet, and to fold the toilet paper six times to wipe one's backside, as any less meant the germs could still get through! (Do they still do this?)

When this training period ended, we were informed where we would be sent for the remaining two years of service. I received the news that I would be sent to join the British Commonwealth Forces, which sounded rather exotic until I read the next part of the letter, which said we were to be based in Korea.

The present population will have a very different image of Korea to the reality that existed in those days when the country had been ravaged by years of war, which had ended – or rather come to a halt or postponement – only three years previously. While it was fortunate that the Korean War had come to a halt, 'incidents' were still regularly reported, such as the death of one of the boarders at my old school that I mentioned earlier.

We were given a few days leave over Christmas before we set sail for Korea, so I travelled to see my mother who had a housekeeping/cook post in a school in Ruggely in Staffordshire. I went by train to the nearest town (I do not recall which one), and found I was too late to catch the last bus, so began to walk in what must have been the coldest night of the last half-century. Eventually, about midnight, I was still nowhere near the school, so I curled up in my Army greatcoat and rested beneath a bridge then continued in the morning to find a very concerned mother, wondering whatever had become of me!

Returning to the Army base at the end of the holiday, we all embarked on our troop ship, *The Dunera*, for our six-week voyage to Japan. (The same *Dunera* that took Franz Stanmpfl to Australia mentioned earlier.) This ship was used for years afterwards, but eventually caught fire and sank.

For some reason, two veteran Staff Sergeants who were in charge of discipline on the ship looked after me, and then enrolled me and another National Serviceman into the ship's Police Force.

I presume they thought we were the only two who had any intelligence – and they were probably right! So there was just the four of us policing the entire shipload of troops. Not all of them were in the Ordnance Corps; many were from a Scottish Infantry Regiment, and as far as I could tell, mostly from Glasgow. In those days, no-one went near Glaswegian soldiers if they could avoid it, especially after an evening at a pub. It was standard practice in all towns and villages situated near Army barracks to ban the sale of 'scrumpy' – unrefined cider sold from the barrel – which seemed to transform the Glaswegians into a genuine 'fighting force'. Naturally, anyone who got in their way, especially fellow National Service soldiers from the soft south, became the enemy.

The strictest rule on board ship was the 'no smoking' rule below deck, which consisted of three tiered bunks and hammocks placed wherever there was space. And there was very little space. This was considered the most dangerous place to smoke on a ship, as of course it posed the risk of the smoker falling asleep. On one occasion when I was patrolling the lower decks, some stupid Glaswegian was smoking in his bunk, so I felt I had no option but to take his name and report him. When he passed me on one occasion later on, he swore he would 'get' me when we got ashore. Another colleague said I should not be too bothered, as he would protect me!

On the way to Japan, we stopped in Tangier and were allowed shore leave, but advised not to take photos of the local women. A taboo. While sailing through the Suez Canal, there is a stretch where there is a road running alongside, and at one point a rough looking Egyptian popped up and started to do some very 'unusual things'! All the soldiers on the troop deck rushed to the side, inducing a very severe list to the ship, and all cheering like mad. The first-class deck, which had been full of wives and 'high ups', disappeared before you could blink. We then stopped for shore leave in Aden, then still a British 'property', and the most unsavoury place one could imagine.

We then passed through the Red Sea. The weather was so incredible that we all slept on deck and enjoyed a marvellous view of the night sky and its stars with crystal clarity. I remember seeing large showers of shooting stars. We then went on to Colombo, capital of Ceylon (now Sri Lanka), but did not go ashore. Instead, loads of traders came alongside, selling fruit, especially bananas. I bought a bunch and was amazed at the taste. Nothing like these sun-ripened fruit had ever been imported into the UK. The next stop was Singapore; again, we could not go ashore, and instead were plied with boatloads of fruit sellers.

The next stop was Hong Kong, where we were allowed shore leave for the day. A few of us went together around Kowloon on the mainland, and then went over to Hong Kong island and travelled to the top of the local mountain using their ancient rail system, which is still in use. At the top there was a spectacular view. There were also lots of young boys who distracted us by their antics and then painted our boots with white paint before demanding that we pay them to clean our boots. We all refused and cleaned them ourselves. Heartless!

We then sailed on to Japan. When we first left England, we were surprised at how good the food was, and in particular some very tasty rabbit. By the last two weeks of the voyage – a total of six weeks of sailing – the rabbits continued to be served, but by this time they tasted quite different. To say they were 'high' would be an understatement. They could easily have propelled the boat on their own.

Finally, we arrived in Japan, in a town called Kure, about 15 or so miles north of Hiroshima. It had a large ship manufacturing base, and major naval base. It was also the headquarters of the British Commonwealth Forces, and to our relief, almost all of us in the Ordnance Corps were to be stationed here instead of travelling on the Korea. The Scottish regiments all went on to Korea, including the cigarette smoker. Huge relief.

We were in Japan for just under a year, doing rather boring paper/clerking work. I have no memory whatsoever of the various jobs I was given to do, apart from one lengthy and apparently very important task. Halfway through my stay in Japan, I was given a special role. It seemed I had been singled out as the brightest of the bunch (believe me, that was not very difficult), so was presented with sheet after sheet containing an inventory of all the Army supplies held in store, collated against another inventory of all the items that had then been shipped over to Korea. My job was to examine both inventories to check that all the figures added up. At least, I think that was the purpose of this exercise.

Throughout my year in Japan, and even before I arrived there, there were endless stories of the Ordnance Corps sending equipment from headquarters in Japan over to Korea that never arrived, or disappeared after being unloaded. These missing items were of every variety, including heavy trucks, tanks, tank spare parts, engines, artillery, and such like. It took me weeks to complete this work, but about three days after I had submitted it, I was called to the Army Headquarters to see the Colonel in charge of equipment – a stern, forbidding Australian, who gave me the impression that he had never smiled in his entire life. He had noticed that in one column the total did not add up. Out of the many hundreds of columns, two items were missing. So I did a check, and quickly noticed that the totals would have been accurate if I had added up correctly! I had missed out just two items. Relief! The Colonel also looked relieved. I was quietly impressed with my own rapid counting skills, but tried not to show it. After this exhilarating work, I was promoted from Lance Corporal to Corporal!

Thinking back on this exercise, at the time and over the years since, I am still amazed that the Colonel had spotted this single error in sheet after sheet of numbers. I was also curious as to why he was clearly so anxious and perturbed at just two missing items in a total inventory running into thousands of pieces of equipment. I have often speculated that all the stories of items going missing while being transported to Korea, or equipment that had gone missing after unloading, had been just myths. This led me to speculate that perhaps the Colonel's evident anxiety when spotting what he thought were two missing items could have been real fear that two items had genuinely 'gone astray', and thus proved the myth was no myth. If so, it would not have been surprising if he had been hugely relieved when he found all to be in order! I will never know. I am sure there should have been a medal for my diligent work, but no, just promotion.

The town of Kure was nothing special, except for its huge shipbuilding yards. I can remember a huge oil tanker, of reputedly around to 45,000 to 50,000 tons, being built in what seemed a matter of months – to be followed by an even larger tanker. Both the speed of construction and the size were far in advance of anything the UK was able to build at the time. Already in 1956, the seeds of British industrial decline were obvious to see.

Kure was also frequently visited by the USA 7th Fleet. This huge flotilla of warships would dock for rest and recuperation every so often. While we never saw the ships, which were hidden by the dockyard buildings, we all knew whenever they arrived. The clue to their arrival was the vast numbers of young females, who must have come from all over the country, forming exceedingly long queues outside the dock gates. They must have been offering exotic Japanese sweets.

The rest of my stay in Japan was fairly uneventful, except for two periods of leave. On one, I went for a long weekend to Kyoto, the ancient capital, which was full of old buildings and shrines and temples, and it seemed to be the centre of their silk industry. I bought two silk ties that I still have! Another week's holiday was spent in Tokyo, staying in an holiday home run by American evangelists. I could not believe the quantity of food they served up, especially at breakfast. Coming from an England just out of rationing, it was astonishing to see the table piled high with boiled eggs, poached eggs, fried eggs, bananas, grapefruit, melons, pineapples, and lots more. Most of it was left uneaten.

About six to eight people were staying there, mostly Americans. After the evening meal, they always held a prayer meeting, when everyone had to kneel in front of a chair and pray. One youngish American girl, who was extremely well bolstered front, middle, and back – and made at least three or four of me – kept screaming into her chair, pleading for the good lord to save her from a very particular sin! I could not help thinking she need not bother, as I was sure there would not be that many men, if any, willing to assist. The problem for me was that I was in agony attempting to stifle howls of laughter, and the only way I could stop was to literally swallow a cushion to the point that I was almost choking. I lasted out... but only just.

What I found most disconcerting was when I boarded a bus. This was in the days when most Japanese would not have had much contact with Westerners. I was taller than anyone else on all the buses I travelled on, and not by just an inch. I was made to feel at least five feet taller than any of the other passengers, such was their curiosity. Obviously, that's an exaggeration, but in addition I had red hair among a population of only black-haired Japanese. I must have been a true museum or zoo exhibit!

Another weekend leave was spent in the beautiful resort of Myajima, an island in the bay of Hiroshima. This was an old Japanese resort and had apparently been requisitioned by the USA forces for what was called 'rest and recuperation'. We were also allowed to visit, to recover from our onerous office paperwork.

One very uncomfortable visit I made was to Hiroshima for a day trip. The city had already opened the museum of the Atom Bomb and its aftermath, which was very disturbing. The museum was near the famous 'shadow' that could be seen on the pavement behind where a pedestrian had been standing at the time of the explosion. It appeared as a consequence of having been shielded from the explosion by an unfortunate pedestrian, and therefore was less bleached than the rest of the area. Nearby were the remains of the church that stood directly below the explosion, and which had been left as a memorial. It still stands unrepaired to this day As for the rest of the city, there had been some rebuilding along the main road, but little else, except for what looked like temporary buildings.

Back in Kure, the shopping area consisted of one side of a long main street, with all the shops seemingly guarded by young women, and where everything seemed to be exceptionally cheap. I saw what to me seemed like a beautiful crockery set, costing £6.50! I bought it and sent it back home. It went to Anna, and after her death came back to me. I also sent home two bolts of silk, again for pennies, hoping they would be made into something. But they never were. At least one of them resides in our chest to this day. Well, we are always told it is the thought that counts.

Eventually, in October 1956, our time in Japan was over. Reflecting on this experience, it was an extraordinary insight into a very different community. The sight of the shipyard and the speed with which huge vessels were being built was a foretaste of just what the Japanese industry would be capable of. The shipyard was just off the main road into town, and we had a clear view of the men building the ships. I never once saw any worker ever stand still, nor even walk slowly in their concentrated and intense labours. The same was true of all other workers, such as street cleaners, builders, and even office staff. No employee in the large office where I worked – and there were many – ever stopped to have a chat, smoke, or ever looked up for contemplation. Unlike us; including the office boss, a very senior Sergeant Major. The only exception to this was when any Japanese worker managed to stick a pin into their fingers while collating paperwork. They did not respond well to pinpricks.

To my disappointment, we were sent home far too soon. We embarked on a converted and very elderly Norwegian cargo ship that took us to Singapore, again via Hong Kong. I cannot remember if we were allowed ashore, but I think not. Soon after we passed Hong Kong, we ran into a heavy storm, which caused me an embarrassing problem. The food on board ship was awful and there was not much of it, so I was constantly starving. Any opportunity I had, I ate bread – as it was the only food item of which there was a good supply – and what I thought was butter. However, this resulted in me eventually spending a few hours being violently sick. It was clear afterwards that my vomiting was food induced, rather than seasickness, and that that the butter had been anything but. This was the only time at sea that I was ever sick. It was also the end of my bread and butter consumption.

We then ran into another storm. What was interesting was that during what was quite a violent sea, everyone stayed hunkered down below deck, while I climbed up to the highest deck above the bridge and thoroughly enjoyed the storm.

A day after we left Hong Kong, an officer on the ship told us that the UK was at war, having invaded Egypt and the Suez Canal. It was not the best news, and we all thought that since we were already travelling, and had all our gear, it would be natural to send us to join the invasion. But we went to Singapore instead, where we stayed for three weeks. I did some sightseeing, but judging from photos of the place now, what I saw must have vanished.

The weather in Singapore was incredibly hot and humid, resulting in all our gear becoming covered in mould within a few days. Another memory was of a swimming pool situated in the officers' (and their wives') quarters. We were allowed to use this facility, but as soon as you got in, you immediately got out again. The water stung our eyes – the reaction of chlorine and pee!

We then embarked on a Norwegian-owned ship that was not fuelled by rabbit. It took us back home, but as the Suez Canal had been blocked by the Egyptians, we had a lovely trip, stopping at Cape Town, and Santa Cruz, Tenerife, and were allowed onshore at both places.

In Cape Town, we had been warned not to walk into certain parts of the town which were preserved for the black community. There were no notices that told us where these boundaries were, so three of us who went ashore together found ourselves straying into one such area. Three black men, who had been walking on the other side of the road, saw us and crossed over in front of us. They then walked a few feet ahead and, in turn, let out some very loud farts before continuing on their way, howling with laughter. We left as quickly as we could. We then had shore leave for a few hours in Santa Cruz, Tenerife, which was an interesting place, but we did not have enough time to fully explore.

A rather sad reflection on the British soldier was the state of the Norwegian-owned ship by the time we reached England. A ship's officer explained that it had been used for years to transport mainly French, but also Belgian and Dutch troops, all of whom would leave the vessel in good order and with minimal damage. But by the time we returned to England, the ship and its furniture were in an awful state. The damage must have run into thousands of pounds. Maybe all the soldiers had discovered an effective alternative to cider and decided to make up for the fact that there had been no proper fighting while they were in Japan.

All in all, my trip to Japan was a wonderful experience. Together with the two sea journeys, it proved to be a lovely, all-expenses paid world cruise, and an almost year-long holiday in Japan, which had been hugely educational.

Arriving back, we were assigned to our next base, which for me was Bicester, near Oxford, until I ended my period of National Service in September 1957. This establishment housed huge warehouses of every sort of Army equipment. Our job was mundane and boring deskwork, which involved despatching various bits of equipment to other Army units and then endless stocktaking.

I was assigned to an office headed by a very laid-back Staff Sergeant who appeared to be in perpetual rivalry with the only other Staff Sergeant in the building, who took life very seriously. But however boring life was, I flourished! I made the dizzy heights of Corporal, and was given most of the seriously important jobs such as walking to the warehouse, counting the packets of whatever (such as pants), and checking that the paperwork matched up. One such stocktaking exercise was to check whether there were still 100 socks stored in the warehouse. Very difficult and taxing.

There was a second full-time Army Sergeant in the office who had fought in the 2nd World War – or so he said. He was certainly old enough to have done so. I was never sure just what he did, as he never seemed to do anything. But neither did the Staff Sergeant in charge. I had the distinct impression that if any job needed to be done, I did it. I began to find this somewhat tiring, literally so, as there was really never that much to do. But what there was, was given to me. Since these few jobs interfered with otherwise very little to do, I had become unused to working hard – or to put it into the vernacular, I had become rather lazy.

I vividly recall one moment in that office. The Staff Sergeant brought in a newspaper; I think it was the *Daily Mail*. On that particular day, it had printed a quiz. So the office – consisting as it did of this Staff Sergeant, the Sergeant, one other Private, and me – sat down to do this arduous but clearly important quiz. I should recall that this was still in the politically fraught period following the fiasco of the Suez War/invasion/stupidity/call it what you want, started by the Prime Minister Sir Anthony Eden. The entire military had still been on alert for months since the abortive invasion. Even after it was all over, Sir Anthony Eden's name was almost a daily constant in the news and newspapers, so it was impossible to ignore or be unaware of his existence. However, this quiz had one desperately difficult question, namely: Who is the Prime Minister? The Sergeant could not answer; he did not know. Unbelievable, but true. All these years later, as I write these memories it is clear that nothing much has changed.

One diversion was a three-week course in Field Craft, after which we were examined, and I achieved the highest score. However, one highlight, or lowlight, was that this course involved training in the use of bayonets. This had not been part of our basic training, and given that the Ordnance Corps is not a frontline fighting unit, was possibly just a fill-in to kill time. Nevertheless, bayonet training we did. However tough or weedy the individuals were – and there were quite a few of both – nobody found it easy. All we had to do was approach a propped-up sack filled with straw, and plunge in our bayonet. It sounds easy, simple even, yet it was anything but. None of us managed to plunge our bayonets more than a tiny fraction of an inch. Physically, it had to have been easy, so that was clearly not the problem. The problem was psychological. Not one of us could do it until we'd had much more practice, and even then, only one or two (not me) could plunge the bayonet more than about one to two inches into the sack. If the exercise had been real and when it mattered, perhaps self-preservation would have enabled us to kill the enemy before the enemy killed us, but this preferred option would not have been at all the likeliest outcome. But then, we were not from Glasgow. And not filled up with scrumpy cider.

At the end of this three-week course, the unit had a 'passing out' parade day, and as a reward for gaining the highest marks, I was assigned the task of leading our group in the parade. (None of my marks were obtained for the efficient use of a bayonet, but for things like knowing where to find 'North' on a compass.) But this meant I had to take the parade, i.e. I had to march out in the front and give all the orders. This was difficult enough, like barking out 'left turn' as we reached the end of the parade ground, and the only way was 'left'. We also had to march with our rifles, which were still the old-fashioned 2nd WW Lee-Enfield's that weighed a ton. And with all the weight being taken on the right hand, I had a problem.

The evening before the parade, we were all given the evening off, which inevitably meant a visit to Bicester village – and a pub. Having spent the evening in the pub, it was natural that we had all been drinking a bit too much. On the way back, some drip in our unit decided to wind me up, and continued when we got back to our barracks. Eventually, I got fed up and hit him on the jaw. He was much bigger than me, but it shut him up – and broke my thumb.

I did not dare say anything about my poor thumb, so went ahead with the parade the next morning, out in front of the unit, shouting out the orders which were complicated – like 'left wheel, right wheel, halt' and 'stand at ease' –while wielding this rifle that weighed a ton, and trying not to display any sign of having a problem. I succeeded, and nobody got so much as a hint that I had taken this parade having received a serious combat injury the previous evening.

Like everyone else, I went on leave for the weekend. I went to London to stay with Florette who took me to Hammersmith Hospital to get my thumb sorted. After three weeks' sick leave, I returned, and ended my National Service in September 1957 with no further combat injuries.

I had kept in touch with an old school friend, Patrick Edwards, who had finished his National Service at the same time, and we met up afterwards and reminisced and kept in touch for many years. Much later, he was my Best Man. He joined Margaret and I on a holiday trip to Austria and Northern Italy in 1971, and in later years we met intermittently, until his much too early death in 1997.

Author during National Service in Japan. 1956.

CHAPTER 6

From National Service to university

When I got back to England, and before the end of my National Service, I knew I had to start thinking of my future. I'd had an ambition to get to university, and gradually began to entertain the idea of studying psychology, but I was not going to succeed in obtaining a place on the basis of my 'A' level results, so I had to wait to apply later on as a 'mature' student.

To fill in time, I found a job in a library in Forest Gate, East London, and worked there for about 1½ years. It paid the rent and gave me continuous and easy access to books in a very well stocked library. I found accommodation with a lovely family, who also rented out a room to another student. One advantage of these 'digs' was that the husband worked in a fishmonger's shop in Forest Gate, and so would regularly bring home fish of a quality I had never previously encountered. His wife was an excellent cook, so I never went hungry. Those were the days when the typical local café/restaurant cook still believed in overcooking just about everything, especially cabbage, which ended up as mush. The only restaurant/café in the area near the library was an aficionado of such mush, named as cabbage on the menu. But perhaps this was not as bad as a very live maggot I found one day, just emerging from a nut in a bar of Cadbury's Milk and Nut Chocolate.

It was good to have a job, but the actual work was incredibly boring, as it consisted of booking in or booking out the borrowed books, and at the end of the day putting all the books on the shelves in their correct place. But at least it was work and kept me in funds. Those were the days when one could walk into almost any shop, factory, or office, and be taken on in one capacity or another. But this library job seemed the best option at the time, as I knew – or at least hoped – it would only be temporary.

Another member of the staff was married to a man who was employed in some management capacity at the nearby massive Ford car factory in Dagenham. Those were the days when the Ford workers had an appalling reputation for coming out on endless strikes. This created a fairly difficult situation, as anyone who had the slightest interest in trade union and factory politics knew (if he/she wanted to know) that the other large vehicle factory just to the north of London at Luton, namely Vauxhall, never had any strikes, and continued not to have strikes until a very minor problem in the late 1990s, if not later. Why the difference?

The right-wing press constantly criticised the 'Communist/Stalinist/Leninist/or was it Trotskyist' supporting trade union workers, and would always crucify the unions for 'bringing out' the workers. What no newspaper in those days ever remarked upon was that Luton's Vauxhall workers, who were all similarly unionised, never went out on strike. Funny that! The concept of 'good management' never crossed the minds of the average *Daily Telegraph, Daily Mail, Times* or other right-wing reporter and commentator, nor Conservative politicians. Nothing much changed in the following years when the British Motor Corporation factories were being constantly called out on strike by their leader, 'Red Robbo' – to Margaret Thatcher's continued fury. Again, all the blame was invariably heaped upon 'the workers'. If any of these ignorant politicians had studied Industrial Psychology, which of course later became part of my curriculum at university, they should have known that decades of research demonstrated that good industrial management virtually always started at the very top of the management structure, not the top, middle, or bottom membership of the unions. The best-managed firms would rarely, if ever, suffer strikes. Even though I had not yet started my university course, I knew that the universal concept of the irresponsible worker was a myth, and in all probability was a deliberately fostered myth.

To make life interesting, I went to every play put on at the famed Theatre Worksop in Stratford East, run by the famous and influential theatre director Joan Littlewood. These included *A Taste of Honey* , *Oh, What a Lovely War*, *The Quare Fellow*,

The Hostage, and *Fings Ain't Wot They Used t'Be*. These were all fantastic productions, but sadly very poorly attended. The problem, I suspect, was that Stratford East was quite a long distance to the east of the West End Theatre district in London. The West End was posh; the East End was not.

Another activity I undertook was to go to an evening course, 'Understanding Music', which was a series of classes that concentrated on chamber music. I also entertained myself by joining a dance studio, earning a Bronze Medal in ballroom dancing. The Army did not hand out medals for my 'active service' in Japan, so this medal was, and still is, a well-earned substitute. Unfortunately, it did not come with a ribbon.

In the summer of 1958, my mother, Toni and I decided to enjoy some mountain climbing, so travelled to the village of Vent in Oeztal, Tyrol, for a mountaineering trip. We hired a (elderly) guide who had taken my Aunt Florette and Uncle Franzl on the same trip the year before, and which had given us the idea. We stayed in a hotel in Vent itself, the last village in the valley, situated approximately 6000ft. above sea level. And after a few acclimatising walks, we climbed another 3000 feet and slept overnight in our first mountain hut. In reality, these are huge hotels, with shared dormitories and, mostly, superb food. (This was the same mountain hut/hotel that we were to stay in overnight in 2001 – see later.)

We arrived after a long slog, ate, and then settled into our dormitory. But we were asked to remain very quiet, as a young man in a room next door was very ill with pulmonary oedema – an affliction that is more common in much higher altitudes – and a doctor was attending him. The next morning, we were told he had died.

We began our four-day tour by climbing the Wildspitz, the second highest Austrian mountain. The first half hour or so was spent walking comfortably along a flat path to the start of the climb. When we arrived at the base, we were given crampons, roped together, and began to climb a huge ice field. It was steep. It was very steep! To say I was nervous would be an understatement! We got to the top of the ice field without slipping all the way back down, and then had another long slog to get to the very top peak.

We then managed another two mountain peaks on successive days, one of which, the Fineispitz, involved climbing up a steep knife-edge to the very top, and which was covered in hard ice all the way up. I dared not look over the edge, as this would have meant leaning over too far to see anything, and I was sure I would slip and fall down my side of the edge, or fall over the other side of the edge into the abyss. Terrifying! But much worse was on the way down, as we then saw how far it was to the bottom, and the edge appeared even sharper and more precipitous on either side. The guide was an old man, who would not have been able to hold us if we fell. To make it worse, two elderly, doddery women had attached themselves to our group. We all, thankfully, got back in one piece.

I do recall one amusing incident, when one young lad looked in awe at my boots. I had used my Army boots, which I had had converted by getting a shoe specialist in London to fix climbing studs along the outer edge. This lad was most impressed.

At the end or our tour, we walked all the way back down to Solden – the next village, but a very long way. The weather was hot and stifling, and when we arrived, we all drank gallons of apple juice. Never has apple juice tasted so good. These days, this route is a well-made wide road, but then it was a rough track.

My memory is that I walked down to Solden with my mother and Toni, but in my mother's account, she said we had sent Toni down to Solden in some transport. There was certainly drama on the way down. After maybe half an hour, we were walking along a narrow stretch of the track when I heard a very loud crack high above us. I looked up and saw a huge lump of rock hurtling directly towards us. Halfway down, this rock hit a projecting rock, and broke in two. One still very large piece landed about 3-4 feet directly in front of us, and the other equally large piece landed 3-4 feet directly behind us.

So many 'what ifs'! What if it had not split in two? If we had been walking a fraction quicker? If we had been walking a fraction slower? We certainly came closer to death that day than at any other time since the wartime V2 rocket decided to take a close look at our garden in Woldingham, before deciding to kill two cows instead.

At the end of this trip, we spent some time in Innsbruck before returning home. I had given in my notice at the library, and with the help of an aunt, Franzi Pirquet, I found lodging in Fulham in an apartment fronting the Thames belonging to an Austrian family she knew. I was then recruited to do lots of odd jobs for this aunt, for which she paid me. This included teaching English to a group of Austrian au-pairs, despite the fact that I had never previously taught anything to anybody.

A few words about this aunt. She was one of two daughters of my grandfather's eldest brother, Theodor. Franzi Pirquet was described as a human dynamo, and I was told she had been largely responsible for rescuing the Sacred Heart nuns in England during and after the war. I am not sure if this was a formal arrangement, or whether it was her dynamism that led to her taking over informally. However, she had the reputation of basically having rescued the Order from collapse. I have no idea to what extent this was true, but that was the story being told. The flip side of this was that she managed to get everyone to do what she wanted, even if they did not want to. She succeeded by her sheer force of energy and personality, or as some would call it, by bullying. Nobody could say 'no' to her. She simply did not understand its meaning.

But I have to acknowledge that it was basically her efforts that propelled me to university, for which of course I was, and still am, supremely grateful. In the end, I could not wait to get away and end her heavy-handed application of what she thought was good for me. She was right, but being at the receiving end of forceful help (bullying) was difficult.

Before I went to Reading University, I had passed my driving test, after my aunt had paid for my driving lessons. And I found a job delivering TVs and other electrical goods for J & M Stones, a huge home electrical goods company with over 200 countrywide branches. (It later became Civics, which finally collapsed just a few years ago.) In a matter of a few months of driving the branch's delivery van, I had three minor skirmishes with its metalwork, one of which involved getting my driver's side door hooked up in another car's front bumper while carrying out a reversing manoeuvre. The door was a sliding one, so I thought I would disentangle it quite easily by simply driving forwards. And this worked. The door freed itself from the other vehicle... and then disentangled itself from its owner, the van, and ended up falling onto the road. Humiliation.

The branch where I worked had managed to gain more sales than any of the other group's stores, year after year. But I discovered one example of how they managed this feat. The main salesman sold a 'brand new' radiogram (a combined radio and record player), which was very expensive. This was in June, and I had to deliver it. Within a few days, though, I had to collect it. The owner returned it in disgust after he had discovered remains of Christmas tree needles in the back! The solution was simple. The salesman who had sold it as new cleaned and polished it up, and put it back on the market again – as brand new! It sold. The third time it had been on the market as new!

The apartment block I was living in was just a short cycle ride from the Chelsea football ground. I had always been a Chelsea Football Club fan from my time at school, but had never had the chance to go to any of their matches until I started to live in London. While living in Forest Gate in east London, I had managed to get along to a few games. One in particular I will never forget, but not because of the match itself. Until then, I had always lived in the south of England, and only ever heard the local southern pronunciation and BBC English. But on this occasion, I took the underground train back to Forest Gate, and managed to find a seat. As the train filled up, a group of giants boarded the train, stood towering over me, and began to speak a strange foreign language. It had to be foreign, as I could not understand a word. I thought it might have been from one of the Scandinavian countries, though I was not sure just which one it would have been. Then came sudden enlightenment. The match had been between Chelsea and Newcastle!

When I first went to Chelsea, the entrance fee was 2 shillings, paid at the turnstiles (no booking needed), then after about two years the price went up to the outrageous sum of 2 shillings and sixpence! But I managed to see the introduction of Jimmy Greaves, the best forward Chelsea and England has ever had. I still recall seeing the best goal I have ever seen, scored by him. In all the many years since of going to innumerable matches, I have never seen a comparable goal. To indicate just how good he was, in his first year at the club as a junior he scored over 100 goals while in the reserve team.

While all this was going on, my aunt had another job for me. Just another of her activities was to arrange for Austrian girls to come over to work in the UK as au pairs, and she insisted I should teach them English! I cannot imagine that they learned any English from me. In addition, she thought it would be a good idea if I myself studied for the Cambridge University exam in 'English for Foreign Students'. I passed one of the papers with distinction! But as I had become fluent in English since my arrival in this country in 1939, I was not particularly impressed.

I had applied to study at a few universities, but the University of Reading invited me to sit for an exam as a 'mature' student (being 23 years old, I was very mature). This entailed a visit to the university and writing two essays, but no interview. I succeeded, and London County Council gave me a maximum grant for maintenance and tuition.

During the six weeks or so before the start of the university term, I decided – or Aunt Franzi arranged for me (I don't recall just who thought of the idea) – to spend the summer in Graz, Austria, with the Minutillos. Claudia Minutillo's father was a first cousin of my grandfather. The arrangement was that they would have me for the summer in return for me teaching English to their second son, Toni. The father was the head forrester to the Bishop of Graz's estate, which seemed to cover a huge expanse of the province of Steirmark (Styria). The holiday was fine, and to this day on the very few occasions I see Toni, he says my teaching was effective.

The city of Graz is, incidentally, well worth visiting. One of the au pair's I taught in England lived in Graz, so I was able to travel to Austria with her, and then visit her and her family there. Occasionally I helped out on their farm, taking in the harvest.

Halfway into the holiday, I had an illuminating insight into their thoughts about the war. Claudia, her husband and I were relaxing one Sunday afternoon, having coffee, when she asked me why Churchill hated the Germans so much. I was taken aback, but just said he did not hate the Germans at all, rather he hated the Nazis. Presumably, their attitude was the result of Churchill's unremitting attacks on Germany and Hitler during the war.

This was an illuminating comment for me, as it was the very first time I realised just what an impact Churchill's unremitting attacks on Germany and the Nazis would have had on German citizens, even those opposed to Hitler. What would the British have felt if there had been unremitting attacks on them for beliefs shared only by some of them, but where this distinction had not been made. I imagine it must have been difficult to distinguish the targets of Churchill's continuous verbal assaults against the Germans.

Once again, I spent the last week with Karl and Susie in Vienna, where the most memorable part of the visit was again going to Gerstner Konditorei on around four occasions, always coincidentally at lunchtime. I always had the most delicious lunch, and in particular deserts. This was still in the days when whipped cream was real whipped cream, and not what you get these days –stuff pumped out of some device.

University Rowing Club. author at Stroke seat. (1st rower at front)

CHAPTER 7

The University of Reading, to qualification as Clinical Psychologist

Having come back from Austria, I began my three-year sojourn at Reading University, having obtained a room in one of the university's Hall of Residence, namely St. Patrick's Hall. I stayed in this hall for my first two years and then, with two others, went into rooms in a private house, which entailed us three doing all the cooking and buying, etc. I had never cooked before but turned out to be the best of us three!

Shortly after the start of term, the Dean of Studies interviewed all new students within his faculty. When he saw me, he had clearly read up on my background and history and appeared most impressed with my distinction from the Cambridge University exam in 'English for Foreign Students'. He wanted to know why I did not study English. I had to do some quick thinking and said I thought it would be a good idea to widen my horizons by doing psychology instead. He was even more impressed!

I took every opportunity to participate in as many extra activities as I could. I joined the Rowing Club, becoming good enough to do a few outings with the 1st Eight, rowing in the Reading 'Head of the River' annual race (2 ½ miles) three times, and the London Head of the River race twice, which is rowed in the opposite direction but otherwise the same course as the annual Oxford/Cambridge race – all 3½ miles of it. 3½ miles on the Thames is a long way. Much longer than 3½ miles anywhere else!

I took charge of the publicity for the Reading 'Head of the River' event in the second year. Rowing was good fun but hard work, being especially tough on the hands. Anyone going to a rowing event these days will see ultra-light boats made of the most modern materials available. At a recent Alumni event at Reading, there was a presentation from a graduate who had won a gold medal at the London Olympics. A single rowing boat was on display, and she was able to pick it up with one hand. In my day that would have been impossible, unless one was a gorilla perhaps. The 'Eights' were correspondingly heavier, especially those made in the old 'clinker' method, which consisted of a series of heavy wooden planks. It was heavy even when all eight rowers picked it up. These days, ultra-light material is used, so even 'Eights' look as light as a 'Single' skull did all those years ago.

Heavy or not, the Boat Club was extremely well equipped and was one of the leading University Boat Clubs outside Oxford and Cambridge. However, what was most distressing was the occasional rowing competition between the university and local schools, such as Eton or Radley College (near Oxford). They put up crews rowed by 14, 15, 16 and 17-year-olds. It did not matter how young they happened to be, they regularly beat us, but of course almost all of us had never rowed before we came up to university. Still, it was humiliating.

I also decided to join a small group of two who produced a general interest university magazine, The Kennet Review – the Board consisting of the editor (who edited for one year), and the ex-editor and myself. At first, I looked after the design of the magazine and the organising of the printing with a local printer. Then, in my second year, I took over the editing for the next four editions. Having joined the Catholic Society, I was elected its president in my second year, but I am afraid to say I have no recollection of what I organised or did – probably very little. For some perverse reason, I was also elected to the position of President of The Psychology Society in my second year. Again, I have little recollection of what I did during that year; again, probably very little. It seemed that my age, being five years older than most of the others, seemed to impress my fellow students. This was odd, as there were four other psychology students in my year who were all over the age of around 40. Perhaps they were too old to count.

At that time I was one of the very last national servicemen to go to university, with just a few others being in their last year or who were post-graduate students. Reading, along with all the universities at that time, bemoaned the end of National Service, feeling that the maturity of the students had taken a heavy dive. Of course it did, and was bound to, with school leavers being in competition with ex-national servicemen, some of whom would have been in active combat (including me – see earlier chapter) in the previous years.

I was very fortunate in that my mother's sister Florette, Franzl, and Elizabeth had moved from London to live in Reading, so I used to cycle there every week with my laundry on a Wednesday afternoon after rowing, and was fed there as well. On some occasions a friend of theirs and his children were visiting. In my second term, I decided to grow a beard, and one day when I was visiting and the three children were present, the youngest – about three years old – took one terrified look at my new beard and me then burst into tears. I shaved it off.

During my first year, an enterprising first-year student arranged a charter flight to the USA during the summer holiday, at a cost of around £45 return! I had managed to eke out my grant, so jumped at the chance, writing to my mother's youngest brother Silvio to ask if I could stay with them in Belmont, near Boston. His two children, Flora and Nora, were still very young, and very bright.

I hitchhiked from New York to Boston. Before I arrived, I was told that the family had already booked flights to Austria for their holiday, but instead of putting me off they had invited Otto, an old Austrian family friend, to stay and look after me while I had the task of looking after their dog and a caged bird. A week after they left for Austria, the dog was run over and killed just outside the house, and a week before they returned the bird dropped dead! Otto and I went to the airport to collect them on their return, and when Silvio asked about the dog and the bird, we had to tell them the bad news. We both felt the situation was so ridiculous that neither of us could stop laughing.

Apart from the death of their dog and bird, my stay was great. I managed to wangle my way into being allowed to use the Harvard University Library, which was huge, and I put together some essays in preparation for the following term.

Since I was in the United States, I took the opportunity to visit my father's sister Eva and her husband, Hans Hochfilzer, in St. Paul, Minnesota. I travelled there and back to New York by Greyhound bus, which took a long time but was very comfortable. It had the bonus of travelling via Niagara Falls and Chicago, and at each of these two stops there was a few hours' interval before the bus resumed its journey. I took full advantage of each break by visiting the Niagara Falls, which were far more spectacular than any photo, but I do not recall much of Chicago. It was just a big place with huge canyons between featureless skyscrapers.

The whole week in St. Paul was very strange. Hans picked me up in his beautiful black Buick, and I thought I would be staying with them, but instead Hans had paid for me to stay in the main City Hotel. This included a free pass to the huge swimming pool in the basement. I was told I would be given all the towels and swimming gear I needed, and I was encouraged to make use of it. So, the first afternoon I went down and was given a towel and what looked like a thin facecloth. I assumed some swimming trunks were folded up inside the towel. Big mistake. As I entered the pool, I saw six elderly men at the far end, all wearing a flimsy and very loose, or more accurately, free-hanging facecloth, flopping back and forwards and all heavily occupied, as they walked about. I walked out, and I never went back.

Hans had arranged to pick me up in the evening to take me to their country club for dinner. As we entered the dining room and were taken to our pre-booked table, two very elegant middle-aged ladies were already seated there. We sat down and after what seemed like an eternity but in reality was about two minutes, Eva introduced me to these two ladies and informed them who I was. In doing so she mentioned that I was a nephew of Susie Pinschof, her brother Karl's wife. On hearing this, one of the ladies exploded, saying she knew Susie and showered her with praise, saying she had played Susie in the North-West USA Tennis Tournament around 1934/5. She said that Susie had been representing Austria, and they had both got to the final. On the day of the final, she said that the weather had been exceptionally hot, even by the standards of Minnesota, so that Susie was gradually worn down, even though she said Susie had been well supplied with refreshments by Karl (in contrast to Susie's own earlier account,) and as a result this lady had managed to defeat Susie! *Mea culpa.* What an astonishing coincidence. For those readers with a short memory span, go back to the paragraphs where I recall my stay with Karl and Susie in Oed, Austria.

This was, of course, my first visit to the Midwest of the USA, and I soon discovered that it was very different to the East Coast – the latter being not so different from the UK, at least in comparison with the Midwest. Throughout this meal at the Country Club, this same ex-tennis player used her right hand to cut her meat, then skewered it onto her fork that was held in her left hand. She then transferred the fork to her right hand, after which she transferred the food to her mouth. This went on throughout the entire meal. After a while, enlightenment! I realised what her problem was. She had clearly become paralysed in her left hand. This had to be the explanation, as neither Hans nor Eva copied her! It was much later that I wised up to the fact that this was considered to be the height of good manners and was just one of the many ways the Midwest differed from the Eastern Seaboard!

On another evening, Hans took me out for a meal, and he began to question how it was that the UK put up with 'socialized medicine'. Here was I, explaining to an experienced hospital surgeon the benefits of the NHS. He then commented how awful it was that the UK had to put up with its appalling 'Socialist' Prime Minister, Harold Macmillan! He was a politician who had been wounded in the 1st WW, and later rescued the Conservative Party after the calamitous Anthony Eden, who had been responsible for the Suez debacle. Macmillan was no Socialist, but by today's standards he was a very middle of the road Tory. This was an interesting insight into the politics of the USA.

I went back to New York at the end of the week, again by Greyhound bus, but curiously I cannot recall a single part of that journey. I found a cheap hostel to sleep, and I made sure I locked the room at night! But again, although this was a very cheap hostel occupied by what appeared to be the unemployed, or certainly the very poorest in New York, the range, quantity, and quality of the food on offer was just astonishing.

I spent a few days in New York, which was fascinating, but what I felt outraged about, not having been warned, were the many men who lived on the streets, often fast asleep, half on the pavement, half on the road. Nobody took any notice of them. Unfortunately, not much has changed. I walked for miles sightseeing, through Harlem, up to the northern end of Manhattan, down to the south and passing the notorious Bowery, where most of the homeless slept.

I remember having lunch in a café and ordering fried eggs, only to be asked if I wanted them 'sunny side up or sunny side down'. I had no idea what that meant but said sunny side up. It was when walking along the Bowery that a psychology classmate, John Marshall, who had of course also been on this trip, saw me and ran up to beg £5, as he had run out of money. As it happened, I still had some so I gave it to him, and he did pay me back later! He went on in life to become a well-known jazz and sessions drummer.

When I got back to England, I received a letter from Eva asking why I had not contacted Louise Hutchings, the sister of my Aunt Carmen, saying that she had booked seats for me at the Metropolitan Opera! It might have helped if she had told me she had contacted this aunt. It might also have been useful if she had given me her telephone number and address!

The three years at Reading seemed to be over before they began. I did reasonably well in the finals, enough at least to apply successfully to the Manchester training course in Clinical Psychology, starting in September 1963. (Of course, I would have achieved at least a First if I had not engaged in so many extra-curricular activities. Self-evident really. And this was long before the grade inflation that has taken place over the last two decades.)

The Clinical course was based in what is now the North Manchester Hospital, an amalgamation of the old Crumpsall General Hospital and Springfield Hospital – a psychiatric hospital, where the course was held.

For my first three years I lived in digs in North Manchester's Cheetham Hill district, in a house owned by a Ukrainian family. This suited me fine. They rented out one other room as well, and soon after I had moved in, the elderly man who occupied the room below mine started banging on his ceiling, yelling that I was disturbing him whenever I was writing. It appeared that the scratching of my pen on paper disturbed him. A few days later, he suddenly rushed out of the house screaming and proceeded to run down the road stark naked! He was taken to hospital.

For my first four months I was paid the annual salary of the princely sum of £640! Then after a government enquiry, this was increased for my grade to £860 per annum three months later. Riches. However, money was still so tight that for my next two annual holidays I volunteered to take part in two research projects. One was on the Isle of Wight, testing school children for a research project conducted by the Maudsley Institute psychologists. I am not sure any more why it was done, but it paid, and the other holiday job was invigilating tests in a school in Blackburn, doing a project for something I also no longer remember.

I spent my entire first year at Crumpsall Hospital supervised by Phil Feldman, who had initiated a large research project into the treatment of homosexuality, then still a criminal offence. Men were queuing up, desperate for treatment. (I was not given a choice; it was part of my clinical training.) However, soon after the Labour Government came into office in 1964, the Home Secretary, Roy Jenkins, changed the law, making homosexuality no longer an offence. This was largely in response to the Wolfenden Report. Wolfenden, who chaired this report, had been, and still was at that time, the Vice Chancellor of The University of Reading.

The next two years were spent in the professorial psychiatric unit and then at a children's psychiatric unit at Booth Hall Hospital in North Manchester. The professorial unit had its entertaining moments, at least in the eyes of some. One of the psychiatric lecturers would spend an inordinate amount of time locked in his room with his secretary. Then a trainee psychiatrist thought he would undergo hypnosis, just for the experience.

Afterwards, he was asked if he recalled any of what had gone on, and he replied, 'No, because I was told (while hypnotised) I would not be able to recall anything.'

I got on well with the two psychology tutors employed within this unit. One of them had made contact for a number of years with local boxing authorities, and he carried out psychological assessments on as many retired boxers as he could get hold of. The results showed quite clearly that they all suffered similar intellectual deficits, which could only have resulted from their life of boxing. Whether any similar research has been carried out on the elderly and retired footballers of that era, I am not sure, but judging by all the recent accounts of footballers from the 1950s, 1960s and even 1970s complaining of suffering dementia, it is almost certain that they would show the same intellectual deficits as the boxers. This would not be surprising, given the heavier weight of the football in the past, made as they were of leather, which, when soaked with rain, became even heavier.

I passed the psychology course and qualified as a Clinical Psychologist, taking up my first post as a qualified Clinical Psychologist at Booth Hall Hospital in September1966.

Away from work for a moment, in April 1965 I flew to Vienna for the funeral of my grandfather, travelling on the same plane as my Uncle Peter, my mother's brother. A few years later, probably around 1969/70, he had been out in the field behind his house and, when walking back, collapsed and died.

Having spent three years in digs, I bought a newly-built flat in Prestwich, North Manchester – my very first property. This was a one-bedroom apartment in an estate of similar buildings, with 12 apartments in each block, for the huge sum of £1870. But I loved it. I designed and then took charge of the small front and rear garden and planted them up with roses. Getting a mortgage had been difficult, but the builders sent me to the Leeds and Holbeck Building Society who gave me a mortgage for which I had to pay the exorbitant sum of around £6 a month. The estate was situated to the rear of Heaton Park, one of the largest in the country, and I took advantage of this by often going for early morning walks and learning to identify the huge variety of birds. Margaret and I drove past this estate while on a visit to Manchester in 2020 to find it dreadfully run-down.

After qualifying as a Clinical Psychologist, I obtained a post at the Children's Department where I had spent some of my time training. I stayed for the next two years as a Basic Grade Psychologist. The oddest moment was when the psychiatrist in charge met me in a corridor and stopped me, saying, 'You know, John, we take children into our in-patient ward for six weeks, and when we then discharge them they all seem to have got better, but I have no idea why. I am beginning to think it must be the colour of the walls.' It had clearly never occurred to him that the likeliest explanation was that the children had spent six weeks away from their parents. It appeared that the idea that parenting could be important never seemed to occur to the psychiatric community. Or at least, some would say parenting was important, but if things went wrong with their children, it had nothing to do with parenting. It may not have been in any particular case, but only thorough investigation could rule out any background issues. If relevant investigations were not made, no conclusions could sensibly be arrived at. To me, this seemed like a wonderful example of denial, even by those professionals who were working within the sector. For the public, similar denial operated, but that could perhaps be excused, as no parent would be happy to acknowledge that they might be getting things wrong in their parenting to the extent of causing their child psychological problems. I have more to say on this issue later.

While I enjoyed the work, my family should know that the highlight of my time at this Children's Unit was meeting your respective mother/mother-in-law/grandmother in September 1967, shortly before my 30th birthday! I had been in the staff dining room for lunch, as I was every day, when three nurses rushed into the dining room and fell into their seats, laughing and breathless, and making one hell of a noise! One was Margaret! The die was cast there and then! I discovered she was working in the children's Neuro-surgery ward and so, if my memory is correct, I made some excuse to visit the ward with no doubt some urgent business. We met again at a staff dance a few weeks later, and the rest, as they say, is history.

Shortly after we met, Margaret and her old school friend Sandra took themselves off to Trinidad to stay with Sandra's sister for what seemed like an eternity. They were there for three months: agony.

I had previously often attended concerts at the Free Trade Hall, starting as soon as I arrived in Manchester, at the time when Sir John Barbirolli was its Principal Conductor. For years the population of Manchester and Salford idolised this man, and there were never any unsold seats. After Margaret and I met, we continued to go as often as we could. It was at one Barbirolli concerts that I experienced what must surely be a unique event. Just after he started the second movement of some symphony, he stopped and turned to the audience and apologised, saying he had gone wrong and would start again. He was probably a bit over the top with whisky, which was not unusual.

While I had previously completed the three-year training course and qualified as a Clinical Psychologist, the three year 'In Service' or probationary course in those days was the main route into Clinical Psychology, but with no examination at the end. There were a few university-based courses, which ended in the students being awarded a Diploma. So in 1968, the British Psychological Society started to offer its own Diploma, which entailed sitting some exams and writing a research thesis. Four psychologists entered in the first year, including myself. Of the four, only two passed, one of which was me! While I was swotting for the exam and writing up my thesis, and shortly after meeting Margaret, I fell ill with glandular fever!

It was during this period that a senior psychology colleague passed onto me his regular commitment of invigilating the testing of candidates sitting for the Mensa exam – the outfit that was alleged to discover those individuals with a superior IQ. I looked up the technical details of the test they were using, which led me to believe the claims made for those passing being of very superior intelligence was highly questionable, if not fraudulent, but they paid me to invigilate, and I always needed the extra money. It was not up to me to question the premise of the test.

It was also during this period that I started doing evening lectures for the University of Manchester's extra mural department, in conjunction with the Adult Education Authority. This entailed a three-hour evening period, with a half time break of half an hour. The preparation for these lectures on various psychology topics taught me most of what I remember about psychology. I went on doing these evening lectures, after a few years doing two a week, for altogether 11 years. Though the pay could have been better, the extra income was useful.

It was while lecturing that I discovered a fascinating property of heavy head colds. Very occasionally I used to suffer really bad colds, when I could use up a box of 'man' tissues in an evening. On one occasion prior to an evening lecture, and then on a second occasion when lecturing to speech therapy students, I arrived with the heaviest, most vile head cold that I almost cancelled the lectures. In the event I proceeded, but on both occasions had taken the precaution of arriving armed with a box of 'man' tissues. I stood up to start each lecture, fearing how I would cope, but throughout the evening I never needed to blow my nose or sneeze once. As soon as I got back into my car at the end of each lecture, the 'heavens' opened up again. Reflections on colds and sneezes.

Having completed two years at Booth Hall Hospital, I was appointed Senior Clinical Psychologist for the Bolton Area Health Authority, which was my first experience of being in charge of a department, even if I did not have any other staff to manage. I had also made history in Bolton, by being the very first Clinical Psychologist to have been appointed to this authority! I stayed for four years, working across all specialties: receiving referral of adult psychiatric outpatients and in-patients through child psychiatry; paediatrics; elderly; GPs; and from any other specialty that knew what psychology was. (Actually, not that many!) Half the time was spent working in a child psychiatry team headed by a psychiatrist who was neither the brightest nor the best.

These were the years when child abuse was just beginning to appear above the horizon. I am not sure if we saw any abused children, and if we did, we did not recognise it. However, on one trip to Billinge Hospital, near Wigan – an outpost we were contracted to serve – I had to see a child who had been admitted on a ward. As I entered the ward, I noticed a woman who was sitting on the edge of a bed, 'away with the fairies', but holding whom I presumed was her son and who was wearing only a very short vest. He appeared to be around three or four years old. His mother was gently stroking him where she shouldn't, and continued to do so for my entire visit of about one hour. I agonised over whether I should go up to her and point out what she was doing, but ducked it. I felt guilty about that for years.

Turning away from work, I have already mentioned how I observed Margaret announce herself in the Booth Hall staff dining room. We met again at a hospital dance a few weeks later. We married in 1971 while I was working at Bolton. This is perhaps the time to say that this was the single most important encounter in my entire life.

All that I managed to achieve later could not have been accomplished without Margaret. She gave me a degree of stability that I needed. I hope Madeleine, Lissie, their respective husbands and grandchildren will agree that together we did not do a bad job, but the lion's work and effort was put in by Margaret. How she managed to achieve all she did – namely bringing up two daughters, two years of Open University courses, Manchester University degree, working, and keeping me sane – is beyond me.

In 1971, Margaret and I sold the flat in Prestwich/Middleton and bought a house on a fairly new estate in Egerton, North Bolton, for the grand amount of approximately £7800. Had we made the move a year earlier, the price would have been around £5000 – the difference being a period of huge inflation during the premiership of Edward Heath and the Conservative Party. Nevertheless, it was a good move.

Before the first oil crisis around that time, I used to be able to fill up my VW Beetle for around £4.80s, but suddenly, to my horror, filling up the tank came to the exorbitant total of £5. Difficult to imagine in 2021.

I do not recall having been overworked while at Bolton, but I spent quite a lot of time doing work for the British Psychological Society, being respectively secretary, and then chair and secretary, and chair again of the BPS Clinical Division, North West Branch. We held meetings about four times a year in the major psychiatric hospitals in Lancashire. We were always lavishly entertained at lunch at these meetings, which was a total contrast to the awful institutions they actually were. In one, Brockhall Hospital, the patients on one ward were 'allegedly' lined up each morning and handed the next pair of false teeth that had also been lined up and came to hand! All these hospitals no longer exist, apart from one – the largest in the North West, namely Prestwich Hospital, which at that time would not entertain psychologists coming through the front gate.

I then struck a bit of luck. I put my name forward for election to the BPS (National) Clinical Division and was duly elected to be a member of the BPS Clinical Division National Committee (six places and six nominated!), which entailed trips to London for their committee meetings. This involved train journeys, and initially I used to travel down to London the evening prior to the meeting and stayed overnight with an old school friend I had kept in touch with, Patrick Edwards. He was later to be my Best Man. After three years, the editor of the Clinical Psychologists Newsletter, now called the Clinical Psychology Forum, stepped down, and I took over for three or four years as only the third editor. At the same time, I was always very much involved in the psychologists' trade union, then the Association of Scientific Workers. Again, I recall swapping the role of secretary and chairman for a few years, and holding meetings in the Manchester and Liverpool areas.

Let me introduce a slice of real politics here. Grandchildren, please take note! It was while I was working at Bolton in 1968, and while l was supervising a clinical student, that I had my first insight into the thinking of the far left of the Labour Party. This was the period when entry into the then European Economic Community (later to develop into the European Union} was a real issue, and the Labour Party under Harold Wilson was all for joining for economic reasons. This was when the UK was regularly being called the 'Sick Man of Europe', as a result of its declining manufacturing industries and the resulting ever-dwindling trade performance of the country. These memoirs are perhaps not the most appropriate place to enter into an essay as to why the UK manufacturing performance had deteriorated so badly following the end of its Empire. But deteriorate it did, because of the inability of its industrial managers to realise they could no longer simply export whatever was produced to its old imperial possessions. These ex-imperial possessions were now independent and were able to choose for themselves what and where to buy. In addition, and this is pure speculation on my part, they chose increasingly to do their buying based upon quality and not on nostalgia for the old 'mother country'.

But to my bewilderment, the Labour 'far left' was very much against this developing European Community, as were the 'far right' of the Conservative Party – those dubbed the 'Empire Loyalists' – who in reality could not get over the end of 'Empire' and wanted to prevent any action that might jeopardise the continuation of empire in some form. But then in 1962, the then leader of the Labour Party, Hugh Gaitskell was also against the UK joining the fledgling EEC for similar reasons, saying in one famous speech that joining would end 1000 years of British history. For the left of British politics to be in agreement with the 'Empire Loyalists' on the right wing of the Conservative Party was bizarre.

However, I simply could not understand why the left wing of the Labour Party should be so anti-EEC well into the 1960s and to the present day, given why the EEC had been set up – namely to bind together the European countries that had spent two world wars within 20 years fighting each other to destruction. The idea was that to prevent further disaster, the European leaders wanted – among other goals – to ensure full employment after the catastrophic 2nd World War, as the best guarantee of preventing further conflict. The far left kept on saying the EEC neglected the interests of the working man.

The student I was supervising, Pat Guinan, who I knew to be very far left, told me the reason was that the far left were suspicious that the 'sole' interest of the EEC was one of encouraging the growth of big business and banking. Of course, she was right in this assessment of the motivation of the Labour far left members – apart from the expression 'sole', which omits the consequences, namely greater and greater employment. I had concluded that this obsession of the left was, to my mind, a bizarre misunderstanding of the objectives and motives of the EEC, which has lasted to the present day! They did not appear to understand that it was the economic chaos and resulting unemployment of around 32% at the end of the 1920s that was the direct cause of the rise and election of Hitler.

The concentration on criticising the development of 'big business' by the Labour Left, appeared to show a complete failure to understand the consequences resulting from the collapse of the economies of central Europe in the 1920s and 1930s, especially the unemployment that ran into 32% of the German population as a result of the collapse of the German economy and its business base. After the war, the Europeans understood that it was business of all kinds, big and small, that led not just to an improved economy, but would be a factor that would lead, not just to that improved economy, but also to its consequences of ever-increasing employment. This was the very opposite of the Labour left wing understanding that gave the appearance of believing that employment grew out of trees and had little, if anything, to do with commerce and business of all sizes and varieties.

The later fuss that exhilarated within England after the expansion of the European Union (following the collapse of the USSR and the decision to allow the freed East European countries to join the EU), and its policy of the 'free movement of people', failed to understand just why this policy was so central to the European Union – namely an attempt to avoid small pockets of unemployment becoming larger and larger areas of unemployment, with all its attendant risks. Allowing the workforce in such pockets to move freely to parts of the Union where employment was needed, recognised the conditions within Central Europe – and Germany in particular – in the 1920/30s, and its connection with the rise of Fascism and the 2nd World War. What did President Clinton reply when asked what were the main causes of industrial unrest? 'The economy, stupid!'

I do not know what was in President Clinton's mind when he referred to the economy, but I can only imagine that the European politicians were well aware of the connection between unemployment and social unrest. Whether they were aware of years of research in the field of Social Psychology, I have no idea, but any student within this field of psychology will know of the central effect that the disparity of economic conditions within individual lives has on stability. I would recommend a thorough study of Social Psychology as a basic qualification for all aspiring politicians. This would allow them to appreciate the consequences of too great economic disparities between individuals and communities.

Think of Northern Ireland. This dispute is not, and never was, about religion; it has always been about the unequal economy between the two religious communities. Think of the Black and Ethnic communities, especially in the USA. The Jewish community could be forgiven for thinking that the Nazi Anti-Semitism and its revolting consequences was entirely down to religion, but they would be wrong. The consequences for the Nazi regime of rounding up the Jewish population and sending them to concentration camps and extermination were that it allowed them to confiscate all the Jewish wealth, goods, and property for themselves. Their motives were economic, as has been the motive behind all the various outbreaks of Anti-Semitism over the last 2000 years. This analysis excludes the issue of Israel and Palestine – an issue I will not explore.

To return to the Labour Party and its far left. In my opinion, they should be ashamed of themselves for not understanding the basic motives of all workers in wanting conditions that are not too far removed from the average, no less in Nazi Germany than in industrial Britain. Therefore, they should have always been the main supporters of the European movement, which, despite appearances on occasion, is deeply embedded in the notion of equality within a thriving economy. To anticipate a statement I make later on, the comment of Jean-Claude Juncker, the then President of the European Union after his last meeting with Theresa May, British Prime Minister, was so fundamental to European aims, namely 'the European Union is about peace'. This only comes with economic comparability and stability.

I should also recall here my first encounter with the North West branch of the Association of Scientific Workers, the trade union to which the Clinical Psychology profession were affiliated. As soon as I went up to Manchester, I went to the first meeting of the local branch, which happened to be their annual meeting. I sat there for about half an hour before anyone thought of starting the meeting, but I was able to listen into the conversation of the other five members present. It turned out they were all committee members in one capacity or another. But as they conversed, everyone was swapping stories of their various trips to Moscow over the past year! Eventually, the meeting started, and when it came to electing the officers for the following year, they discovered that there were places for six people. With only six members present, including myself, I was duly elected to the committee!

Over the following year, I heard nothing, and no meetings were arranged until the following annual general meeting. I went to that meeting, and the chairman apologised for not having contacted me, but he said they had no need to have any meetings between the annual meetings because all the issues that arose over the year were at the Christie Hospital in South Manchester, where coincidentally they all worked! Such was the strange state of affairs of our local trade union.

Because the local union branches were so hopeless, when the psychologists working within the Manchester and Liverpool Health regions were discussing how to meet up within the union umbrella, we decided to form a separate branch, which worked well. Over those early days, I served as chairman and secretary a few times, which led to a few trips to London for annual meetings of all psychologist branches in the country. We always met in a hotel in Bloomsbury. One day on my way there, I passed a bookshop that sold *The Little Red Book* by the Chinese Chairman Mau Zedong. I mentioned this to a Liverpool colleague, who left the meeting and rushed out to buy a copy! Such was the very left-wing state of many psychologists in those days, not just the local officials I had come across earlier.

Another slice of local medical politics/nonsense: On my first day at Bolton, I was asked by the Hospital Secretary (the big boss) where I was accustomed to eating for lunch. I said with the doctors (not strictly true), so he duly asked the Psychiatric Senior Registrar, who I knew from my first-year training period, to take me over to the doctors' dining room where he sat me down at a corner table. He then left the room and came back later and sat with the other Consultants. About one year later, after using this dining room together with Pat Guinan – a psychology student I was supervising – I discovered that there had been unease for all that year amongst the junior doctors, first at my presence and then at both our presences. They said they felt inhibited when discussing patients of theirs. Once I realised our presence was not welcome,. I never went back again.

This reminds me of a similar controversy at Hope Hospital, the large general hospital in Salford. Junior doctors had always shared a dining room with nurses. One day, the doctors decided to confront the Matron (the nurses' boss) to say they no longer wanted the nurses to eat in their dining room. The story goes that the Matron replied, 'You don't mind sleeping with them, so you can ****ing go on eating with them.'

Margaret (in centre) while at Booth Hall Children's Hospital, Nth. Manchester

CHAPTER 8

Marriage, and births of Madeleine and Elisabeth

It is time I gave work a rest to mention another important part of my life. I explained already that Margaret and I got married in September 1971, but there were complications of just where we were going to get married. The policy in the church was that one had to get married within the parish where one of the couple resided. We wanted to get married in Minster, Kent, so that my mother could be present, but neither of us resided in that parish.

I need to go back in time here. I already mentioned that my Aunt Franzi had tentacles all over the place, and had alerted my mother to various job adverts over the years. I am sure it was her who alerted my mother to the existence of a Benedictine Convent in Minster, Thanet, Kent, who wanted someone to take over the running of their small guesthouse. My mother applied and became the guesthouse housekeeper/cook in 1958, after our first mountain climbing expedition in Austria. The guesthouse could accommodate about four or five visitors in a building within the convent grounds.

The nuns occupied a building dating from 1027, but the first Abbey/Monastery on this site was founded in 670 AD. Some of the buildings were demolished in the time of the Reformation under Henry V111th. The remaining buildings are now occupied by the Benedictine community who arrived in 1937, the Convent being founded by the mother community in Eichstadt, Bavaria, Germany.

There was not going to be any possibility of my mother coming up to Manchester for the wedding, so we felt the best and nicest solution would be if we married in Minster in the local church, but with the reception taking place in the Convent's guesthouse. Because the Catholic Church stipulated that to get married in a Catholic Church it should be in the parish where at least one partner lived, we had to go to the local Parish Priest in North Manchester and the local Parish Priest in Cheadle (a horrid man), plus the local Priest in Minster to agree. This all took time, but eventually everything was fine. The downside was that most of the guests, including Margaret's parents, brother, and sister, all had to travel down from Manchester.

So, we got married in Minster, with the reception in the Convent guesthouse, with my mother – and no doubt helpers – doing all the arrangements, cooking, etc. My friend from school days, Patrick Edwards, was my Best Man. The Convent – or rather my mother – managed to put on a lovely buffet, together with the best Sachertorte I have ever tasted, before or since, but most of it was gobbled up by Margaret's sister-in-law! To my relief, nobody thought of making any speeches.

We left for our honeymoon with the usual pranks of stones being put into our hubcaps, and headed for the ferry that left from Ramsgate. As we drove off the ferry, we heard another noise: the crew had strapped a long line of empty beer cans to the rear mudguard. How they knew we were just married is a mystery.

We drove to Vienna for our honeymoon, staying there with my uncle and aunt, Karl and Susie. We drove through Germany in wonderful weather, so my side window of our Beetle was kept open from the coast to our overnight stay in Ingolstadt, Bavaria (where they make the Audi cars). At breakfast, while eating a boiled egg, my back suddenly decided it did not want to support me any more, to the extent that I could not even lift my spoon to my mouth. I have no doubt that the open car window was the culprit.

We took ourselves to the local hospital, having made sure to arrange all the necessary insurance with the AA beforehand, and discovered the delights of German healthcare. An officious nun demanding to see our insurance documents confronted us. She did not appear to recognise the AA policy, or more likely did not want to, but said nothing and told us to sit down and wait along with some other men dressed in working clothes. We were kept waiting for ages, while all the time other well-dressed individuals arrived and were seen instantly. Every now and again a door opened behind us, and I could see groups of men (those in working men's clothes) lined up, with a doctor moving from one to another. That was their examination and treatment. Eventually we kicked up a fuss and were seen – and very efficiently, too. Their treatment sorted out my back instantly! But we had to pay. Long live the National Health Service. Thankfully, the AA insurance repaid our costs in full.

We proceeded along the Danube valley and eventually arrived in Vienna. I have very little memory of what we did in Vienna or even how long we stayed. But Margaret saw and was overwhelmed by the magnificent furniture and snuffboxes that Susie's grandparents had brought back with them from China, after being forced to leave because of the Boxer Rebellion at the turn of the century.

We visited my parents' house in Bisamberg, which they had built a few years before the outbreak of the war and then sold to my father's relative, Lotte Leitmeier. During this visit, we were shown round the house, which seemed reasonably sized on the outside, but inside the rooms were diminutive. Lotte showed us upstairs to the bedroom where the upright walls concealed large spaces behind the walls. She explained that there were many occasions when she had hidden fugitives in those spaces while her house was undergoing a routine search by the Nazis. None were ever found.

We walked round the garden, which was full of vegetables, fruits, and fruit trees, one of which, a pear tree, had come from our grandfather's nursery at Hirschstetten. I recall my mother saying this pear tree had been a present from the nursery gardens that her father was responsible for in the family home in Hirschstetten. The pears were the best I had ever tasted, but we were there together with my Aunt Susie who clearly also liked the pears, and we had great difficulty in extracting one from her. Eventually we succeeded, ate one, and took an extra one to take back to England to give to my mother in Minster Abbey. When we got to Minster, the pear was still edible, but when we gave it to her, a guest who was sitting with us promptly pounced on it, and was just about to start eating it when my mother very politely but firmly took it back and explained its significance!

After Vienna we drove to East Tirol, where we stayed at the hotel where the Vienna Boys Choir always go for their summer holidays, and did some climbing and sightseeing. We then returned home via the Austrian Montafon Valley on our way to Switzerland. This entailed driving over a mountain pass, where we stopped to be greeted by a friendly goat that nuzzled the front door of our car. It left a smell, which took many washes to get rid of after we got back to England.

We were camping at this point, and one evening we had a lovely meal after which I ordered a Kaiserschmarrn, an Austrian version of a pancake. We were told this was a main course dish, which we'd already had, but I insisted. That evening, I paid the price, as the entire meal left my guts and was propelled out of the tent into my climbing boots. But the Kaiserschmarrn was delicious.

In due course, we experienced the most important developments in my and Margaret's lives, namely the births of Madeleine and Lissie.

I was present when Madeleine was born and this event was one of, if not the most emotional and marvellous experience of my entire life. I had been allowed to sit with Margaret in the run-up to the birth, but when she was being examined just before the birth, I was ushered out. Clearly this examination involved nothing that mere men should know about. She was then taken into the birth ward, but I was kept waiting outside for ages, in spite of the staff knowing I wanted to be present. In the end, my patience ran out and I just barged in. The staff made no comment and I stayed until Madeleine was born. It was incredible. In fact, 'incredible' does not do justice to just how I felt. I have no doubt my feelings have been duplicated many times by all fathers who have been present at the birth of their child. But it was still incredible.

Madeleine never gave us any cause for concern. She was full of life and energy. But on occasions she found it difficult to settle, and

I used to walk round our sitting room showing her the pictures we had displayed, again and again, until she calmed down.

When Madeleine was about one year old, Margaret and I took a long weekend off and drove to mid-Wales. Each bedtime consisted of me reading Madeleine endless repeats of *The Very Hungry Caterpillar*. I am not sure who enjoyed the book the most; I suspect I did. Just as I was re-reading and correcting this account, it was announced that Eric Carle, the author of *The Very Hungry Caterpillar*, had died, having apparently sold over 50 million copies of the book.

Madeleine was a delightful baby and young child, as was Lissie, who was a very content, eat-and-sleep baby. Unfortunately, just before the birth of Lissie, all the lifting and carrying of Madeleine meant that my back gave out. I could not walk, only crawl. The GP ordered me to rest, so I had no option but to lie down for what in the end was approximately four weeks, which coincided with the birth of Lissie. This meant I could not be present, and our neighbour took Margaret to the local maternity unit when Lissie was due.

When the birth was imminent, I had telephoned the midwife to ask her to phone me as soon as the baby was born. I had been told it was likely to be around midnight. She agreed, so I stayed awake but no phone call came. I continued to stay awake until the early hours of the morning but still no phone call. I was becoming really anxious, so I eventually rang again and was told Margaret and baby were both fine, the birth having occurred soon after midnight. She explained that she had not wanted to ring me with the news as she thought I would be asleep. Naïve does not do justice to this midwife's behaviour. Clearly, I was only the father – unimportant and uninterested. Stupid woman. Margaret's memory is that she phoned me to tell me Lissie had been born! So I am not sure just whose memory is the more accurate. Both may be correct.

The very first time Madeleine heard Lissie cry after she came home, she was terrified! She had clearly never heard herself! Nor had she yet learned how normal that was! But both Madeleine and Lissie were a delight and a huge source of pride.

I must mention the help given us by my mother. Because I could do almost nothing in the final run-up to Lissie's birth, we needed help. Margaret's mother had hurt her neck a few weeks prior to the birth and had a brace around her neck, so we could not ask her for any assistance. So I rang Minster and outlined our problem, and my mother was given immediate permission to come. She became quite an object of interest in the local village shops, as of course she went in wearing her nun's habit or, worse, in her nun's working clothes. Dior certainly did not design them. But she did create a problem. She took it into her head that I needed feeding, so she kept buying cakes and biscuits for me. As it would have been ungrateful and churlish of me to let them get mouldy, of course I reluctantly eat them. And put on weight.

My mother also had difficulty in stifling her own methods of mothering. She clearly thought we were indulging the children when Margaret or I went to them whenever they cried. She clearly wanted to say that we should leave them to cry, as she had done with my brother Toni all those years ago, in the belief that crying exercised the lungs. But she kept herself in check.

In addition to giving birth to Madeleine and Lissie, Margaret later obtained a job at Prestwich for two days a week, studied for an Open University degree for two years, then obtained a place as a psychology student at Manchester University, finishing the course in 1979 with a 2:1 degree. There were big celebrations all round after the end of the Manchester course and a lovely ending with Madeleine and Lissie both pictured wearing Margaret's mortarboard. How she managed the study at the same time as being a mother, brilliant cook, having part-time work, and with me being away so often in the evenings, is difficult to comprehend. She then had a lovely reward as she obtained a post as a lecturer in the University of Manchester's Nursing Department. This Nursing Department had been the first university-based course created in the UK, so its head was the very first Professor of Nursing in the country. I was very proud of her.

We had been living in Edgerton, North Bolton, from 1971, but all the travelling that Margaret had to endure while a student in Manchester became too onerous, so we moved into a lovely, newly-built development in Fallowfield in 1977, just a short bus ride to the university. At last, Margaret's life became less stressful, also helped by our decision to obtain the help of au pairs. This all made our life so much more viable.

I must mention the many lovely holidays we had together. But first, I should mention a day trip to an old Roman settlement near Lancaster. We were sitting having a picnic in a large field occupied by many cows, so there were many 'remains' – otherwise known as cowpats. Lissie was fascinated by them and clearly wanted to explore and see what they really were. We warned her not to step in them, but she insisted. When she discovered that they were not solid, oh dear, did she cry. I carried her to the nearby river and washed it all away.

We went on camping holidays, to southwest Scotland, to the Lake District, the Snowdon area of North Wales, the Forest of Dean, and the Isle of Arran. A storm decided to hit the Isle of Arran just after we pitched our tents, and all the campers had to be evacuated and put up in a local hall. We discovered later that the wind had uprooted one tent, catapulting one of its tent poles through one side of a nearby caravan.

While doing a tour of the island, we discovered the potter, Alastair Dunne, and we bought two small owls – one for Madeleine and another for Lissie. Disaster struck in early 2021 while Lissie was clearing/dusting the mantelpiece and the owl was sent flying. Lissie discovered the owl could not fly. It ended up on the floor, shattered to pieces. I managed to repair some of it, but not its left eye, so Margaret made it an eye patch. We were then able to buy another owl by the same potter, which now looks on and appears to be so sorry for the damaged owl with its eye patch! On another occasion, when camping in the Snowdon area, the weather was so dreadful that in the end we pulled up our tents and went home. This was the only occasion when we allowed ourselves to be defeated by the weather. It was while we were camping in Northumberland that we heard that Margaret's mother had died, so we headed home. While we all knew she had not been in the best of health, her death was still a shock.

One of our camping trips to the Forrest of Dean had its moments! One 'event' ended this particular visit. We were camped next to some woods, but we made the mistake of leaving just enough space for another tent to pitch up next to us. Everything was lovely until a family arrived and duly set up camp in the space we had foolishly left. Judging from their accents, they came from east London, and they had travelled in a large delivery van. They proceeded to unload a large kitchen table and two large kitchen armchairs, then the parents settled down in their armchairs and left a teenage son to look after their 2/3-year-old son. All went well for a while, but I had noticed that the young child often emerged from the wood playing with, and covered in mud. He used to come towards our tent, but I must have somehow signalled to him not to come too close and certainly not to unload the mud.

However, this young lad came out of the wood again, but on this occasion was not playing with, or covered in any mud. What a relief. But, having emerged from the wood, he stood still for a short while. He then inserted his hand into the back of his trousers and proceeded to extract another load of mud! We dismantled our tent and were gone within an hour!

On one occasion, we went camping in the Lake District for a weekend. One evening, when returning to the campsite, both Madeleine and Lissie were becoming very tired and threatening to go to sleep before we got there. We feared they would then not get to sleep when we got back. So I had the idea of telling them to look out for owls. It was quite a daft idea, given how unlikely it was to come across any owls, and even if we did, we would hardly be able to spot them in the early evening half light and in a moving car. But driving round the very next corner, we saw a tawny owl standing in the middle of the road just ten or so yards ahead of us.

Because Margaret was studying and I was working, we needed help to look after Madeleine and Lissie during the day and taking them to and from school, etc. So, as mentioned earlier, we obtained the help of three different au pairs, all of whom came from Spain. First, was a girl called Almadina, then Carmen – who became a family friend – for two years, then Petra. All of the girls settled in and did a wonderful job of looking after Madeleine and Lissie, so it worked well.

As the au pairs went back home for the Christmas holidays, there was one year when Margaret had to work over the festive period, and on Christmas Day I recall cooking the Christmas dinner. And excellently cooked it was. Margaret has no memory of this memorable event.

Both children went to the local infant school. On one occasion, when Carmen was walking the children back home, Lissie told her of an incident at school that day. She said a boy in the class suddenly stood up and said to the teacher, 'Miss, you are a f-----g c---t!' The teacher then dragged him to the washrooms and washed out his mouth with soap. Lissie had no idea just how shocking this would have been to the teacher, as we had not brought her up with such language!

I should mention a painting that Lissie produced while at this school. She must have been about six years old and came home with a painting that we had framed and which we now have hanging in our bedroom. It could be called a painting in the 'primitive style', but to my mind it is the picture I like looking at most. Put Picasso's name to it and it would be worth millions.

Authors Marriage 1971. From Left: Sandra, Patrick, My Mother, John-Margaret, Margarets Parents, Christine.

Margaret at her degree ceremony-front row: 2nd from left.

Elisabeth and Madeleine

CHAPTER 9

Prestwich Hospital/Salford Health Authority (Teaching)

Having nearly completed four years at Bolton in the Senior Grade, I saw a very surprising advert for a job at Prestwich Hospital, in North Manchester. At the time, each hospital was its own independent authority, namely 'The----Hospital Management Committee'. In 1974, the Government reorganised the entire management arrangements of the hospital service by moving all hospitals in a given local authority area into one single management arrangement. Accordingly, two years later, Prestwich Hospital was merged with Salford Area Health Authority. This was a big improvement, as the influence of some of the previous deadwood in the place was partially neutralised. Eventually, power politics from within Salford took over.

However, the advert – which occurred just prior to the NHS reorganisation – was a great surprise, because as far as anyone knew no psychologists had ever crossed its threshold, other than one psychology undergraduate who had worked there as a nurse during his university holiday. This was Phil Feldman, my first clinical supervisor.

The hospital had had 3000 patients at one time, but this had been reduced to just over 2000 when I arrived, although it was still one of the largest, if not the largest, in the UK. I applied and was appointed. Little did I know just what a rollercoaster I was in for.

A short history of Prestwich Hospital sets the picture. A few years after I had started, and after I had appointed a number of psychologists, one of us discovered that the Hospital Library held a copy of a Public Enquiry into the running and management of the hospital dated 1919-1920 or thereabouts. During the 1st World

War, when most of the senior doctors had been called up into the armed forces, a retired doctor had been recruited to run the hospital. The report indicated that he had been appalled at the standard of care and immediately started to agitate for a public enquiry. The authorities repeatedly turned down this request. However, after the end of the war, an enquiry was eventually started and the results published. This enquiry claimed to being the first of its kind. I am not sure if this was actually the case, but it was certainly not the last!

Most of the report was concerned with how the place had been badly run and how the general ethos was years out of date. Two complaints, however, stood out for all of us in the psychology department. The first was the practice of a 'drug holiday' for the patients every Sunday! The second complaint was simply stated, but without explanation. The report commented upon and criticised the practice of 'placing the patients behind the table'.

It was not clear what was implied by this comment. A member of my department, Norma Kelly, asked a senior nurse she was working with if she knew. 'Oh yes.' was her reply. She said that when she had been a student nurse in this hospital in the mid-1960s, she had observed the practice! She described how many wards had huge oak tables. Patients were arranged in their chairs along one wall and these huge tables placed in front of them, so they could not get up or escape, and were often stuck there for hours! It beggars belief, but that summarised the state of the hospital well into the 1960s. One doctor was also still practising the drug holiday on Sundays. I had no idea of this particular history when I answered the advertisement and started the job, which is probably just as well.

A brief outline of the institution as it existed in 1972 will set the picture. The hospital was built on two campuses: one just off the main road on the way from North Manchester to Bury; another second building about half a mile lower down the valley. The second building was a huge Victorian edifice, but built to an incredibly high standard in terms of the fabric. All the huge wards had beautiful teak parquet floors, which must have been worth a fortune. The large oak tables, mentioned above, were no longer huge, but were almost certainly the ones complained about, but radically reduced in size.

The area between the two wings of the hospital had at one time been the hospital farm, but by then was just empty fields. They had possibly been rented out, but I cannot be sure. Otherwise, the ground consisted of beautiful woods.

So, how was it possible that the hospital wanted a psychologist? It turned out that the job advert came about because the Medical Supervisor who had ruled the hospital for years had recently retired! I applied, was appointed, and started at the Senior Grade, as advertised. I knew the post would be eligible to be upgraded to the Principal Grade, but that needed an application to the Dept. of Health. The 'Principal' level was then what is called the 'career grade', meaning this was the highest post one could expect. In those days there was one higher post, but this was for personal achievement such as having many publications, and had no other significance. The manager agreed to approach the Dept. of Health, as I knew he would. The Department of Health approved the upgrading of the post to the Principal Level, as again I was confident they would. So I felt good!

Initially, I had no particular expectations of the job or any vision as to what exactly I wanted to do. I really began on 'a wing and a prayer'. I hoped, or guessed, that there was an expectation amongst the manager and senior psychiatrist that I would soon ask for finance to appoint more staff. This was an educated guess (though not that much education was needed), because I had been shown a suite of rooms and asked if I felt they were suitable. The accommodation I was offered consisted of an entire two-storey wing adjacent to an unoccupied ward, consisting of 12 reasonably-sized offices plus a kitchen, toilets upstairs and downstairs, and a much larger room on the ground floor. In the course of time we used this room for large meetings, therapeutic/educational films, etc. I decided to accept this offer, but it was not a difficult choice. The management immediately offered to redecorate the entire suite of rooms in any way I liked.

After I started, I arranged to do a tour of the hospital. In every ward I visited, the patients appeared to have nothing to do. I had anticipated that this was likely to be the norm. However, I was not prepared for some of what I saw.

On one ward, I saw a very elderly lady. Asking how long she had been in the hospital, the nurse escorting me said she did not know for sure, but thought she had been admitted as a young girl in about 1918/19, and in all probability she had been admitted because she had been pregnant. This reason for admission was commonplace in those early days. Another elderly woman was walking around the perimeter of one very large ward again and again. When I asked how often she did this walk, the reply was 'all day and every day, probably since she was admitted around the 1920s'. This was, of course, almost impossible to verify, as the nurse would not have been working in the 1920s, but if not totally accurate, it could have been pretty close.

The large nursing staff consisted of many three-generation family members, which made reform difficult, as the younger generation would find it hard to criticise the out-dated procedures of their parents and grandparents, even if they recognised out-of-date practice. Their definition of treatment was to dish out the daily drugs and keep the wards clean and locked. All the patients were well and truly institutionalised, no longer having the ability to do things for themselves and depending totally on the staff.

Shortly after I started, I discovered why there had never been any psychologist appointed to this establishment prior to my appointment. This revelation occurred during a formal opening of the new 'Addiction Unit', for all types of addictions. I was invited to the opening, which was being named after the retired Medical Superintendent. After a while an elderly, well spruced gentleman introduced himself to me as the recently retired Medical Superintendent. He said he had been told who I was, namely the newly-appointed Psychologist. He then told me, 'Your appointment is, of course, a complete waste of time. 50 per cent of the patients here are schizophrenic, and the remaining 50% are psychopaths and nobody can do anything for any of them; they are incurable. Therefore you will have nothing to do.' This man's attitude was obviously the reason why this hospital had in all probability been the very last psychiatric hospital in the UK to create a psychology department.

A very short chapter on the history of psychiatry is appropriate here, as it explains many of the underlying problems of Prestwich Hospital and indeed of much of psychiatry, even to the present day.

I came across an article by an American psychiatrist soon after I was appointed to Prestwich. It was by Dr J.S. Bockoven, entitled 'Moral treatment in American Society'. Journal of Nervous Diseases, 1956. It outlined the history of psychiatry from around the end of the 1780/90s and provided a very critical commentary on modern-day psychiatry.

The article described a famous publication, namely 'The Retreat', by William Tuke, a psychiatrist, in 1813. William Tuke had created and been in charge of 'The Retreat'. He described the treatment regime within this small psychiatric unit in York, which claimed great success in the treatment of patients. In reality, these were mostly middle-class women who needed a bit of rest and recuperation and who continued to do their own cooking, cleaning, etc. while undertaking therapy. It was what would later be called a 'Therapeutic Community' for the unhappy or the 'worried well'. When the results were published, it caused a sensation by claiming to improve the condition of psychiatric patients, until then thought to be incurable.

Psychiatrists drew the conclusion that as this particular unit had successful outcomes, institutions were clearly marvellous and the way to go. So, more psychiatric hospitals were built. But then, to accommodate the (apparent) demand, they began building bigger and bigger psychiatric hospitals, influenced as they also were by the parallel development of larger and larger general hospitals in the USA. These latter large hospitals were possible because of the then modern developments in medicine, particularly in anaesthetics.

What psychiatrists failed to appreciate was that in a general hospital, patients were discharged after a few weeks and went back to carry on their lives. While in hospital, they were cared for by nurses, fed by nurses with food prepared by an army of cooks in central kitchens, with catering staff having bought the food.

There were also cleaners for the wards while patients were bedridden for the few weeks after an operation or other treatment. But then, most patients were discharged back to their homes, so were not in hospital long enough to lose their motivation and skills in looking after themselves when they returned home.

So, as soon as large psychiatric hospitals were developed, the ethos of the small therapeutic community, such as at the York Retreat, was lost. There appeared to be no understanding of the short period of time within the York Retreat or in the new large general hospitals, nor any understanding of the actual psychologically-based therapy that patients had received. Instead, patients remained in these new, large hospitals for years and were housed within huge wards, with hospital staff necessarily employed to do the housekeeping chores, cooking, buying, etc. On a purely practical basis, it would have been difficult and impractical for 30, 40, or 50 patients in a ward to cook, clean, etc. for themselves. But after they had been kept in hospital for years and years, they lost their ability and motivation to manage these everyday tasks for themselves. They simply deteriorated and were often so exasperated that they became violent, and they were then locked up in a side ward and/or put in strait jackets.

Psychiatrists assumed that the failure to get people better was due to their untreatable 'mental illness', but in reality was, for a significant majority, almost certainly due to a significant extent to the belief of psychiatry with its model of 'illness'. Hence the comments of the recently retired Medical Superintendent to me after my appointment, which I mentioned earlier.

This kind of regime led to 'institutionalisation', i.e. becoming dependent on the institution for everything. Patients simply deteriorated and were then ever more difficult to treat, because the conditions that led to their initial problems were magnified as a result of years remaining in the institution with little or nothing to do – all because psychiatry had misunderstood the implications of the York Retreat. That misunderstanding had continued into the 1970s and still exists within parts of psychiatry to the present day, including within the field of children and adolescents. The article quoted above, written by a psychiatrist, called this misunderstanding of the York Retreat methods and results 'an historic mistake'. For years, mental hospitals were truly 'mad houses'. Fortunately, this began to be realised – slowly at first in the late 1970s, and with increasing pace in the1980s, with the gradual closing of these institutions and transfer of many patients into small community-based homes.

The above is a very brief outline of the Bockoven article. A full reading of the original article is highly recommended for anyone interested in this important topic and, in my opinion, should be compulsory for all staff employed within this sector.

I should mention that in the 1970s quite a few articles and books were written on the subject of institutionalisation. Their view was that institutionalisation was caused by the buildings within which the patients were housed. My view was, and still is, that the buildings were only very partially responsible, insofar as they made it difficult for patients to look after themselves, such as obtaining their own food and then doing their own cooking, because of the sheer impracticality of 30 to 40 to 50 patients in a single ward having access to a kitchen. But it was then the staff within the hospitals and wards that translated these limitations into actual ward procedures. Thus, staff became acclimatised to taking all the big decisions and, in a sense, became institutionalised themselves. They could not alter time-honoured practices, and called the patients 'ill' for no longer being able to be self-sufficient –the very stuff of institutionalisation.

A major development within the field of mental Illness occurred within Clinical Psychology as this new profession developed in the late 1950s. Until then, the main contribution of psychology within the field of 'mental Illness' was the administration of psychometric tests. It was psychiatrists who thought psychometric tests were useful, probably because they had no sensible treatments but thought that the application of extra psychometric information and labels somehow added to the sum of knowledge. The problem was that this extra information did not provide much, if any, useful extra information, other than in the field of learning difficulties, where such interventions by a small group of psychologists, such as Peter Mittler, transformed and revolutionised the practices within that specialty.

Thus, in the late 1950s, the world of 'mental illness' saw the introduction of psychologically-based 'behavioural therapy' based upon the academic study of learning, i.e. how individuals learn while growing up, such as the learning of living skills, attitudes, motivation, culture, as well as academic learning. Psychologists recognised that many of the problems psychiatrists had been treating with medication, i.e. Illness-based, were in fact caused by consequences of stress, living conditions, prevailing attitudes, parenting, trauma, etc., and which were essentially reactions, or learned, and could therefore be treated by purely psychological methods which attempted to achieve change or 'unlearning'. This was, of course, the antithesis of the 'medical model' of illness.

After I qualified some years later, I became aware that some psychologists appeared to fail to understand the implications of these psychological developments and appeared to proceed on the basis that some 'mental illnesses' could fortuitously benefit from psychological approaches, while remaining fundamentally a mental 'illness'. This is an issue still prevalent, in my opinion, in many children's treatment centres. I have more to say on this issue of child treatment centres later. Clearly, there are individuals who are 'ill', such as some depressions that simply do not respond to psychological treatment and will only respond to medication, sometimes over a considerable period of time. I have had experience of attempting to treat individuals who were referred for what the referring doctor assumed was some psychological/emotionally-based reasons, but who completely failed to respond to, or even comprehend any discussion. The issue for the professional is in being able to distinguish the background causation and not for psychiatrists to assume that all are 'ill', nor for psychologists to assume that all are 'reacting' to some past problem/event.

However, back to the 150 years of the misreading of the York Retreat study and its consequences. The view that psychiatric patients were untreatable informed the practice within Prestwich

Hospital and the beliefs of the recently retired medical superintendent mentioned earlier. A few initial problems may be 'illness' caused, but even then, if individuals are incarcerated for years on end, normal psychological processes such as institutionalism applies to them, adding to the mental illness of those who were indeed truly ill. The sheer frustration of being more often than not locked up in wards with little activity of any meaning led too often, as already mentioned, to the explosion of patients and the subsequent use of the 'straight Jacket' and the locked padded cells, still in use into the 1960s.

I was never going to agree with this medical model for essentially non-medical problems, and my and my staff's entire efforts over the years at Prestwich were intended to overcome this misinterpretation or misunderstanding of the true background and condition of the individuals being treated. Hence many battles and underlying tensions over this period and ultimate denouement!

Problems started soon after my appointment, as I discovered that some of the psychiatric consultants (they eventually totalled six) had the usual very out-dated view of the contribution of psychology, and at least one of them appeared to have no idea what psychology was. The new senior consultant, who was responsible for the psychology post I filled, had ideas formed in the 1950s, before the development of psychological treatments. He had qualified in the days when psychology was very new to the NHS, having only developed in the late 1940s and 1950s, and when their main contribution was carrying out psychometric tests. As I have already commented, none of these tests contributed anything of practical use outside the area of mental handicap, but psychiatrists found them useful as they added to the various diagnostic categories of psychiatric patients in the days when their only contribution to treatment was prescription of drugs and provision of a label. It was truly a madhouse, and I was expected to comply.

I refused. This led to a few arguments with the senior psychiatrist. He had wanted me to carry out those psychometric tests which he had become used to 20 years previously when he was a junior doctor. They were pointless then, and nothing had changed since. This argument ended by me saying that as I had been appointed as the hospital's very first psychologist to head up this new department, I presumed the hospital wanted me to provide an up-to-date psychological service, and for me to decide what that was.

I stuck to my guns, and eventually I think most came to accept what we were doing. Well, possibly! But in the meantime, this psychiatrist must have had a quiet word with the Chairman of the Hospital Board, who invited me to lunch one day. I thought this was a novel but nice gesture on his part, and was in order to meet and get to know this important new recruit to the hospital! But very gently and diffidently and in coded language (that I understood), he suggested I should do what I was asked to do by psychiatrists. I said no (but ever so politely, in equally coded language, and equally diffidently, which he clearly understood), and I was never pestered with this issue again.

I cannot omit an account of one of the psychiatrists, who shall remain nameless. He was a very pleasant, warm, and human individual, but who had his own problems. This was a great shame as he was good at his job, given the standards then prevailing, and probably one of the most human and sympathetic psychiatrists in the region. Soon after my appointment, I went to his weekly ward rounds, attended by an army of psychiatric nurses. The consultant welcomed me and then asked me what I earned. I made up some salary, and he then announced to all the nurses that he earned more!

Even before I was appointed, and indeed even before I applied for the post, I knew that on my own I would not be able to achieve anything worthwhile, so I would have to increase the staff establishment. The offer of the building with its many offices told me that this was likely to have been in the minds of the Authority and Manager all along. This assumption was correct.

The first developments were to obtain finance to appoint three psychologists, starting with Joan Farrell, then Norma Kelly, and then Stuart Bellwood – the latter sadly passing away in 2020. These three colleagues were to provide the bedrock of the department's work and offered me huge support. I never heard them criticise or complain, at least not to me, and I could not have achieved anything without their support, dedication, and expertise. I have mentioned these three because they were the three earliest appointments, but all subsequent colleagues provided dedicated support and their own exceptional service and input. Any difficulties and failures were mine alone, and I do not recall any problem that was due to any of them throughout my time at Prestwich.

The message that I took from the funding of these additional posts was that the Authority had accepted the priorities and practice of psychology that we wanted to provide, and so I took this as a cue to work up a long-term development plan for the next ten or so years, outlining all the various psychology specialisms that should be developed, the number of staff required, and the appropriate starting grade and eventual final grade. However, as I was writing this plan, the Authority that had appointed me had been merged with the much larger Salford Health Authority. I submitted my plans to the newly-enlarged Authority, but my plans were never acknowledged, and I was never even thanked. I was slightly 'miffed' at first, but over time this outline plan became reality in most of its details, albeit with a few changes and additions to reflect other developments. Acknowledged or not, my very ambitious early plan had, in the end, been largely accepted, and thus I felt vindicated.

For about my first three to four years, I had always been invited by the Personnel Director to lecture to all new staff, from nurses to cleaners and all in between. I tried to instil in them the idea that patients were people first and foremost, and on the whole they were receptive. But after a while, I stopped receiving the invitation to do these talks. I presumed they had become too toxic for some of the powers that be, i.e. the Salford power brokers!

We grew steadily after these first three appointments, ending up in 1978/9 with a filled establishment of 18 psychologists and another four in the planning pipeline, with their funding agreed, and around another two agreed and in the planning pipeline, but waiting for funding to be found. This became in all probability the largest, or equal largest, department of clinical psychology in the country, vying for top spot with the department in Exeter.

However, we attracted quite a few critics along the way, with one amusing example occurring around 1975/6 when we had just six members of staff. A senior nurse was heard to explode, saying that wherever he went in the hospital all he ever encountered were psychologists. This, from a nurse – one of around 200! We had well and truly made our mark!

As part of our work in the hospital, we decided to introduce a number of rehabilitation programmes for long-stay patients, among them one run by Norma Kelly and another by Stuart Bellwood. Both were granted demonstration status by the Department of Health – an accolade leading to staff from other hospitals visiting and learning from them. In 1974, the department put on a whole day symposium on the role of psychologists in rehabilitation for long-stay patients, which led to psychologists from all over the country attending. We had established a national reputation.

As the department developed, all the psychologists became very much engaged in providing psychology lectures to staff, and particularly to the student nurses. We ran a whole programme of lectures to the newly-appointed psychiatric nurses, but a big problem quickly became apparent. We were asked to run one course of about ten or so lectures every year, but there were two nurse intakes a year – one at the beginning of the year, and the other halfway through the year. So one year we lectured to the nurses when they were starting their training, and the following year we had some starters, plus some who had by then completed half a year. Nurses who were new were extremely receptive, but the 'old hands' had become accustomed to the old-fashioned psychiatric practices and did not appreciate different ideas from us.

Along with the many internal lectures we gave, I had been asked to give regular annual talks to retiring police officers. This came to an end after I made the mistake of quoting research that showed that those who retired to some coastal resort, never having any connection with that place prior to retirement, tended to become lonely and depressed. Unfortunately, quite a few in the audience immediately said they had bought their retirement homes in just such places. I was not invited again!

The rapid increase in the department led to some jealousy among other psychologists in the region who headed up departments that had remained static over many years. One or two of them were in informal contact with one psychiatrist in particular who worked at Prestwich and who had not always seen eye-to-eye with my priorities, i.e. I did not serve his needs above all others! I may not have, no, I did not learn all the necessary diplomatic skills that were necessary to keep him happy. And this led to some interesting but stressful times from about 1978 onwards.

A service that we helped to pioneer was to provide sessions within GP practices. The argument for this was that many of those who would now be referred to us within the GP practices would otherwise have been referred to Psychiatric Out-patient services and often admitted into acute wards, prescribed medication, and thus establishing for them the idea that they were 'ill' instead of having a psychological/emotional type of problem. There were many occasions over the years of seeing clients who had been prescribed medication by their GPs because they had no access to psychologists, and these patients were then much harder to treat.

We developed these GP-based services without gaining the consent of the management – not having asked – but no-one complained, or perhaps nobody in the hospital ever knew.

This development did not occur out of the blue. The genesis went back to my very first few months after my appointment. I wrote earlier about how I had attended a ward round of one of the consultants after my appointment. This was within his 'acute' unit, where typically adults would be admitted after referral to the consultant from a GP. The typical length of stay within such units could be from a few weeks to a few months, but the facility was not meant to contain long-stay patients.

I attended a few ward rounds and accepted a few referrals for psychological treatment during the first few months after my appointment. However, while all the referrals I saw were in fact highly appropriate and appeared to respond to psychological treatment, the beneficial effects tended to be undone when they returned to their ward. They were not 'ill' in any conventional meaning of that word, and they did not need medication. They did, however, have a variety of emotional problems that medication was never designed to cure. Psychological treatment could and mostly would have been beneficial, but as they returned to their ward, the entire psychiatric model was repeated, treating them as 'ill', nursed, and continued to be prescribed medication. This had the effect of undermining a psychological model and re-instilling the idea that they must be 'ill'. After all, medication is for the treatment of illness or medical ailments.

The conclusion I came to was that the benefits of psychological treatment that concentrated on their real-life emotional problems and difficulties were all undone for the remainder of that week by the application of the medical model by the consultant, junior doctors, and psychiatric nurses. All were doing a good job within the remit of their training, beliefs, and practices of psychiatry, but undermined a psychological approach.

Therefore, there was little point in seeing in-patients for psychological treatment. A much better approach was to see individuals *before* they were referred to the psychiatric services – hence the development of providing psychological services within GP surgeries before they were ever referred to psychiatry. We ended up providing sessions within four or five GP practices, all of them having previously been heavy referrers to Psychiatry. I think we did actually make a big and beneficial difference to treatment and prevented a considerable number of what would otherwise have been hospital admissions. GPs certainly valued the service, which I believe was one of the first such service, or possibly the very first, in the NHS. This was a well thought-out development that of course had its consequences for acute wards – the only area in which the two politically influential psychiatrists had any interest.

Had we had many more staff we could have provided a bespoke service of a psychologist working within an Acute Ward and nowhere else, when the main aim of our presence would have been to influence the nursing staff as much as seeing individual patients. This was certainly within the long-term plans that I had produced, but these developments never came to pass. Time intervened.

But this GP initiative and its consequences for our non-presence within acute psychiatric wards was to prove a major factor, possibly the only factor, that led to long-term consequences for myself and every psychologist in the department, which I mention later.

While my department was valiantly attempting to bring some up-to-date practices into the institution, the hospital received two high-powered visits from experts – one from civil servants within the Department of Health, and another group who were Department of Health-appointed psychologists, seconded from the US Massachusetts-based MIT Institution. The latter group were interested in all aspects of the hospital's organisation. One question they put to me was how many committees there were in the hospital. This was of interest to them, because any psychologist interested in management issues will know that the more committees there are in any institution, the more confusion and contradictions there will be. I undertook the task of finding out, together with the Personnel Officer – a very competent individual. We started out thinking there may be about ten. To the best of my memory, we ended up with the figure of 43! This management expert had then wanted to discuss how such an absurd number could be cut, but I do not recall anything changing. The place was just too set in its ways. His comment on this, and his overall judgement of the hospital organisation, was that it was bewildering.

I can recall an interesting meeting with the Civil Service visitors, who again were there in an attempt to improve the management of the hospital. I had a number of meetings with them, and at one I bemoaned the fact that were was so little for the patients to do and what a shame it was that the old farms in all of the big mental institutions had been closed down. Their reply was that 'closing them down was the only way open to the NHS to prevent the nursing and other staff from stealing the produce. Nothing else had ever worked.' I do not think I need to make any other comment.

An interesting development occurred in 1976/7. Margaret had commenced her psychology degree course in the department led by Professor Reason at Manchester University. I had met Prof. Reason before, and this contact – plus, I believe, Margaret's entry into his department – led to him asking me to put together a course of lectures to be given by my department for his 3rd Year psychology students who were interested in pursuing a career in Clinical Psychology. These were counted purely as extra-curricular lectures for the students. However, these students were obliged to write an essay on topics we had provided. We then had the task of reading and marking their essays. It was hard work, and nearly all were of a very high standard. I do recall being startled and amazed at the quality of one essay in particular. It was exceptional. Fortunately, this student did go on to a career in Clinical Psychology.

I had also been asked to provide a number of lectures to Salford University students as part of the university's extra-curricular input. In addition, at some point during these years, I had also been asked to provide a course of lectures on basic psychology to the university's Speech Therapy students. The students were all very receptive, and though I am reluctant to admit it, much more receptive than the psychiatric nurses we lectured.

For the sake of balance, it has to be said that such a lot has happened for the better within the field of psychiatric nursing that most nurses these days would be horrified at the practices in the 1970s.

In 1975, when Madeleine was three years old and Lissie was 12 months, Margaret obtained a two-day a week nursing post at Prestwich, but in the medical ward of the hospital for psychiatric patients with minor physical problems. I remember her being shocked at the low standard of general nursing provided by the psychiatric nurses. This appointment was only possible for Margaret because the hospital had established a nursery for the children of hospital staff. So, each day we took Madeleine and Lissie to spend the day in this nursery, freeing up Margaret's time. For them, it must have been a very long day.

There was a problem with this nursery. A so-called experienced children's nurse had been put in charge, but she was still living in the Victorian age. On one occasion, when I went to pick up Lissie at around 5pm, she was still sitting at a table with half her lunch uneaten in front of her. The nurse told me that she had wanted a drink and would not eat until she had had a drink. They did not allow this, saying that all food should be eaten first. I was very proud of Lissie. She had stuck to her resolve not to eat until she had had a drink. I immediately gave her a drink and took her home, furious and appalled. I complained to the hospital manager who had in fact created this facility, and although he also disagreed with this nonsense, I do not think he felt able to do anything.

On another occasion, I was called out from some committee meeting by the nursery, as they said Lissie had had an accident. She had fallen and cut her lower lip. It was a very small cut, but this ex-children's nurse did not know how to deal with it! Should she send her to Casualty, or apply a plaster? A plaster was applied. Lissie still has the scar. On another occasion, she praised Madeleine, saying that if she got upset she would take herself off to a corner to cry. Oh dear. Just what were the staff doing? Just sitting and watching the children in their care cry, offering no reassurance?

Another problem was that this nurse manager had an issue with breast- feeding mothers. She did everything she could to sabotage mothers from coming over to breast-feed. Both Joan and Norma suffered from this idiocy, but nobody could change the nurse's Victorian attitude.

I could not complete this account of my time at Prestwich without saying a few words about a difference of opinion that took place between the Professor of Clinical Psychology and myself that was eventually to involve the Salford Authority. This was a pivotal issue, and the outcome led to major changes in my job and in our family lives, and in the lives of all my psychology colleagues.

A Professor of Clinical Psychology had been appointed in the mid-1970s to run the Clinical Psychology training programme. The appointment was highly irregular, as it had been at the instigation of the Professor of Psychiatry, over the head of, and without any consultation with, the current head of the existing clinical course and, as far as we knew, without consulting the Manchester Regional Health Authority who financed the existing Manchester Regional Health Authority Clinical Psychology Course with its base in North Manchester's Springfield Hospital. To add insult to injury, the new professorial-led course was to be housed in the Psychiatric Professorial base in South Manchester. This left the Springfield Hospital Regional Training Department with nothing more to do. It took the work of the existing Head of Training away from him without any consultation. It left the new premises, built to house the training course, high and dry. I have often been told that this event was fairly typical of university politics. I had always thought NHS politics took some beating. Nothing I experienced in the 50 years that I worked as a Clinical Psychologist could compete with this outrage.

This led to huge unrest amongst the region's psychologists, but the deed was done. When the newly-appointed Psychology Professor established a management/advisory committee to help with the running of the Clinical Psychology course, it caused me a dilemma and crisis of conscience. I had admired the original head of the course. Among other attributes, he had appointed me to the training scheme back in 1963! So, should I take part in the newly-established committee advising the new professor and his training scheme? A number of psychologists from other departments took part, so I decided to accept an invitation. This had been a difficult decision, given how the post had been established and the degree of anger within the region, but I felt I had no option if I was to protect the interests of my department. We wanted and needed to be sent clinical trainees from the course, just as we had from the earlier course, to be able to provide the students a useful experience and later to hope they would then apply for any permanent posts within the department. This decision of mine actually worked, as we were sent students as part of their training, and all of them subsequently applied for and were appointed to permanent posts.

Everything went well for about two to three years. However, eventually a contentious issue arose, resulting from very limited funds for clinical psychology training. The Professor had wanted to increase the number of Clinical Psychology students but, with no funding to expand, suggested we should appoint one or two self-funding students. I opposed the idea, along with at least one other member of the committee, because of the likelihood of bias leading to the appointment of someone who was not really up to the standard required but who had the sole merit of having their own funds. I was not sure if there were any formal policies within the NHS that were of relevance. So I took a decision that was to prove fateful.

I wrote to the local union officer to ask for advice as to whether the NHS did in fact have a ruling on the issue. Instead of writing back to me as I had asked, he sent a letter directly to the Professor, saying that the union objected to him going ahead with his proposal. I had been sent a copy of this letter by the union officer and noted that my name had not been mentioned. However, the Professor put two and two together and decided I had been the person who had written to the union officer. All hell was let loose. My professional assessment and diagnosis was that the Professor became very 'unhinged'! Not a diagnosis I was ever to use for any NHS-referred individuals.

The Professor wrote a bizarre letter to my Health Authority, accusing my department of being incompetent in all sorts of ways and of housing a group of trade union Marxist agitators. Or it may have been Bolshevik, or even Leninist, or perhaps Trotskyite agitators – or even all four! I cannot remember the precise term of abuse. There was much more idiotic content, which over time I have forgotten.

I was offered a copy of the letter in order to prepare a reply, but I was told that on no account was I to reveal any of the contents to my staff, as the letter was confidential, being the property of the Authority. I declined to accept a copy, as I knew it would in all likelihood have leaked. I replied but do not remember just what I said, other than to object to all of the comments. The problem created by this external interference rumbled on and on, and it was almost impossible to resolve. But while this external interference was very stressful, I also knew that I had the full support of the Authority's Senior Medical Officer in all that we had been doing.

The difficulty was just how to find a solution to this interference. So, in order to try to resolve this issue, I arranged a private meeting with two of the NHS's most senior and experienced Clinical Psychologists, during the Annual Conference of the British Psychological Society, to ask for advice. One was the current Clinical Psychology adviser to the NHS; the other psychologist having been the ex-adviser to the NHS. Having explained the problems my department and I were facing as a result of this external interference, they suggested that I ask Salford Area Health Authority to make a formal request for help from the NHS. The Authority agreed, and an NHS team came and did sort out the mess.

The NHS team advised that the Authority continue to develop in the way we had been planning but within the officially designated Area Health Authority Psychology Planning Committee, at which the Area Medical Officer should be present. I did hear later that although I came in for some criticism from this interfering Psychology Professor, I also came in for extensive praise from some of the Prestwich consultants. One in particular had told the visiting NHS team that my contributions and conduct and diplomatic skills within our hospital committee meetings was, and I quote, 'brilliant'. I suspect I was more astonished at this comment than anyone else! But modesty leads me to accept that endorsement.

Fortunately, I had always had a very good relationship with Dr. Veitch, the Area Medical Officer of Salford Area Health Authority. The NHS advice was accepted, and with Dr. Veitch attending, we carried on with our pre-existing Development and Planning Committee. However, all proposals for advertising and appointing of new staff, in line with the development plan that I had first proposed years earlier but refined and brought up-to-date, were now put on hold by the Chairman until the Authority had formally endorsed the plans, and until the Head of Department post at this new 'top grade' post was filled. This decision was, of course, perfectly in order and appropriate. This new post was the post I had in fact been occupying for years but paid at the old Principal grade.

Our development plans were approved anew and officially endorsed by the Salford Area Health Authority, and the new top post advertised. Interestingly, I had been invited to the meeting of the Health Authority when our plans were placed on the agenda. The Area Medical Officer and his deputy were naturally also present. I had anticipated that I might be asked to comment on our proposals, and I mentioned this, but the Deputy Health Officer quickly whispered to me to say nothing when the topic came up. The topic did come up. I said nothing. The Medical Officer and his deputy said nothing. The plans were approved 'on the nod'. So that is how things got done.

The newly-created Head of Department post was duly advertised, and of course I applied, along with three other candidates – one of whom was an old friend and colleague. He had been in constant behind-the-scenes contact with the interfering Psychology Professor in all he did, and in constant contact with our psychiatrist who had introduced me to my first meeting on his acute ward by comparing his salary with mine. I presumed this psychologist also knew about, and presumably also supported, the bizarre letter to our Authority mentioned above. He got the job!

The distraught Area Medical Officer came to me immediately after the appointment, very upset, saying he had argued and fought for me to get the job for the entire two hours it took to decide the appointment. He said he constantly referred to my application, containing as it did the entire development plans that had been agreed, and containing as it did all the agreed projects and listing all the developments that had taken place since 1972. The two external assessors, who were responsible for the decision, included the Professor of Psychiatry – the same one who had caused such distress in the way he had created the Clinical Psychology Professorship over the head of the incumbent Head, of course, and who had then appointed the present incumbent. The other assessor was an old colleague of this Clinical Psychology Professor! Such were the shenanigans up North.

I had had no illusions about the prospect of my being appointed as soon as I knew the identity of these two external assessors. I was even more certain of the outcome during the interview, when it was clear that they were obsessed by my department's withdrawal from 'Acute' ward rounds mentioned above. Nothing else was of any concern to them. I attempted to explain the decision, but sensed it was a forlorn exercise.

I was upset about the decision for about an hour but then decided life must go on. Salford, however, agreed that I had been acting up within this new grade for at least the past two years (actually, since I was first appointed), and they paid me all the back-wages at this new higher level for the period. Quite a substantial sum! Satisfaction of a sort.

After he had started his job, the new head came to see me and pointed out that it would have been unlikely for me to have been appointed after the 'investigation' into my department by the Department of Health. I was surprised at this comment, and I told him that I had initiated this visit. When I showed him the letter I had written to the Medical Officer with this suggestion, he was very put out, upset, surprised! He said little after that, and I never saw him again.

I was reminded later that I was apparently overheard to ruefully remark, though I do not recall this, that perhaps I had misheard or misunderstood the earlier remarks of the previously retired Medical Superintendent after my appointment in 1972, namely that when he had been referring to the 'untreatable' schizophrenics and psychopaths, he had in fact been referring to external colleagues, not patients.

Because it was clear to all in the department that I would be looking for another job, Stuart Bellwood left before I did to take up a job in the South. After some months, I applied for and got the job of Department Head for the Maidstone Health Authority Psychology Department. This, of course, led to massive changes in our lives.

It is interesting to speculate on what would have happened had I obtained the new post within Salford. I will comment on some of the consequences later, but I never regretted the various decisions I made during my time at Prestwich. I am sure, no, I know, I could have been more diplomatic at times, but the various developments in terms of our involvement within the hospital and our service development to GPs would have been much harder to achieve and perhaps, for some developments, impossible if I had been more experienced when I took up the post and as a consequence had sought agreement for all our developments.

Another way of summarising my time at Prestwich is to say that I did what I did and took the decisions that I did, all for sound psychological reasons, but some of them may have been ahead of their time. I am sure some might say I was naïve. If I had my time again, being appointed to the hospital at the same time in 1972, with the same history, but crucially with the benefit of the experience I had obtained over all those years, I doubt if I would have achieved half of what I in fact did, purely as a result of knowing how difficult it would be and so avoiding my style. Or in other words, being much more diplomatic.

I was never sure just what all the members of the department felt about the outcome of me going. I never asked. Perhaps it was better not to know. But in all the years at Prestwich, I never received any complaints or criticisms from my psychology colleagues. I certainly felt that I had always had the full support of all the staff. I can recall just one staff issue, when some within the department asked me to speak to one of their colleagues about his personal hygiene! I did so, and it did have some positive effect.

After I left, it was not long before Joan, Norma, and Amanda also found other posts as heads of departments, and I was delighted to have been asked to provide a reference for each. They each deserved an exceptional reference and they obtained one. I felt a lot better.

All the other psychologists I had appointed also left, and I was told that the new department head floundered in the post. He died after a few years, as did another old friend of mine who had supported the interfering Professor, and as did the Professor himself a few years later. I doubt there was a connection between their machinations and deaths.

To complete the story of my activities during the years I was at Prestwich, I edited the BPS Clinical Psychology Newsletter for three to four years in total, and we managed four editions a year. It continued to develop over the following years into the current 'Clinical Psychology Forum', published monthly.

Another activity I was involved in, that entailed travel up to London, was to be a member of the Department of Health's Principal Psychologists Committee. All new Principal Psychology posts throughout the NHS had to gain approval from this Committee before they could be advertised. Only if they followed certain management arrangements did they gain approval. Membership of this committee consisted of two NHS representatives, two BPS Clinical Division representatives, and two union representatives. I was one of the two union representatives.

This whole arrangement officially followed, but actually slightly predated, the publication of the NHS 'Trethowan Report'. I had been involved, with two colleagues, in writing draft proposals for the management arrangement of psychology departments, which were later endorsed completely by this Trethowan Committee. These included, among other proposals, the important detail that Principal Posts, the then career grade (later Top Grade posts), could only be approved if they were established within an 'independent' department, i.e. not headed by a psychiatrist. This was hugely controversial among a few psychiatrists, even though the principle had long been established in some areas, including in Bolton and Prestwich/Salford.

Publication of the Trethowan Report had been held up for some time because of opposition from one psychiatrist who sat on the committee. But the Department of Health was in strong support of its conclusions and remarkably set up this 'Principal Psychology Committee' in advance of publication and formal approval. So we on the committee began to implement the proposal concerning the necessity for psychology departments to be independent before any new Principal Post would be approved. This single advance was to be hugely significant for the continual development of psychology within the NHS.

When going to these regular meetings in London, I invariably visited the National Design Centre's Exhibition Centre in the Haymarket, near Piccadilly Circus. I always came back with some small present for Madeleine and Lissie. I liked them, but I am not sure just what impact they had on Madeleine and Elisabeth!

CHAPTER 10

Maidstone and Maidstone Health Authority

Returning to the problems at Prestwich and with the external interference, not only did I not brood for long, but instead, the outcome of not getting the new post resulted in probably the best move I ever made, however fortuitous and unintended for myself, Madeline, and Elisabeth – but not for Margaret. She was the major loser.

Getting a job elsewhere in the Southeast, in Maidstone, starting in September 1981, had some long-term repercussions, which were all to the good with this one exception, which was serious. This major downside to moving away from Manchester involved Margaret. She had to face the great disappointment and sacrifice of giving up her lecturing post within the prestigious Manchester University Nursing Department, which quite rightly meant so much to her. As I previously mentioned, it was the first such University Nursing Department in England and headed up by the first Professor of Nursing in England. So, leaving was clearly a huge wrench and sacrifice for Margaret, but I never heard her complain once. In fact, the very first time I heard her speak of her disappointment was very recently, while writing these memoirs. I am not sure I could have remained silent for so long if I had been in her position. Let me correct that statement. I *know* I could not have remained silent for so long.

Was my application for the position in Maidstone selfish, giving little thought for what it meant for Margaret? Probably. Would I have been able to obtain a head of department post in the North, near enough for Margaret to be able to remain in her post and so not needing to give in her notice? There were no such posts advertised then or later that would have been appropriate or near enough for Margaret. My new salary was much higher, and however justified or unjustified, that was an important factor for the long-term future. So I applied to the first suitable advertisement, which happened to be Maidstone.

We can never know what the long-term outcome would have been for the future job prospects of Margaret, or of Madeleine and Lissie, had I obtained the job in Salford and we'd stayed in Manchester, but their future would hardly have been the actual outcome that emerged after the move south.

Which brings me to Madeleine and Lissie again. I don't recall any problem with either throughout their childhood, although they were very different. One interesting difference showed itself while we were still living in Manchester. I used to lie down and cuddle them when they went to bed, and I alternated which one I would cuddle first. If it were Madeleine's turn to be first, I would have great difficulty in extracting myself in order to cuddle Lissie. She would always say, 'No, don't go yet.' Eventually, I would extract myself and go to Lissie. After about 30 seconds, she would say, 'You can go now, Daddy'! What had I done? I did ask her once why she had 'dismissed me', but she said she did not remember! Perhaps she does not remember, but perhaps---?

But back to our move to Kent and its long-term implications. First, Madeleine would in all probability not have met her husband Chris! Thus, there would be no Annabelle or William. Similarly, Lissie would in all probability not have met her husband Marcus, and hence there would be no Sam or Rosa. Life without these marriages, respective sons-in-law, and their respective children, would have been enormously diminished. The enlarged family has made the life of Margaret and myself immeasurably more rewarding than it would otherwise have been.

The move to Maidstone was not trouble-free, though. We managed to find a buyer for our house in Manchester quite quickly, but our buyer was ensnared in a chain that took time to unravel. Thus, from October 1981 to Christmas, I lived in a hospital flat during the week. The hospital authorities, however, interpreted the NHS guidelines for such circumstances very generously and paid for me to eat out each evening. I suspect that my absence over the weekdays did not suit Lissie, who fretted, even though I commuted back to Manchester each weekend. The relevant NHS rules allowed me to travel First Class!

Shortly after our move to Kent, I was amazed when I received my first request for the payment of council rates. While in Manchester, I recall the rates for the council and water being near to £980 per year. For some reason, I had not enquired what the local Kent council and water rates would be before we bought our house. Perhaps this was because I feared that living in the prosperous South, the rates would be far higher than in Manchester. They came to around £350 a year. I just could not believe it... at first. But it soon became clear just why the rates were so low. The provisions within the County of Kent, especially concerning education facilities but also Social Services, were wholly and disgracefully inadequate for all the population needs – other than for the top 10% of the population, who gained places in the local grammar schools, and the very wealthy population who felt they had little need for any local authority services. This low rate was evident to anyone who cared to investigate.

After Christmas, I managed to get accommodation for all the family in a hospital house. The house was divided into two apartments, and we were given the choice of which we preferred. We inspected the ground floor apartment first, only to find the bathroom sink was half eaten away with what must have been vomit. No doubt a leaving present following a party. We chose the top floor apartment. This had also been left pretty dirty, but the hospital housekeeping team did a (fairly) good job in cleaning up. But Margaret was alone during the day, which I suspect was not the best of experiences for her.

The move to Maidstone meant a new school for Madeleine and Lissie, which was initially a temporary arrangement in the local Barming Junior School. The headmaster was very welcoming, as he came from Manchester.

A plus side of moving down to Kent was that we were much closer to Minster and my mother, who by this time was beginning to display very slight symptoms of confusion. Not yet serious, but noticeable. Prior to this move, we used to drive down to Minster from Manchester, which entailed at least seven hours' driving, initially through London as the M25 had not been completed. But now, living in Maidstone, the drive down to Minster was just short of one hour.

The long drive down from Manchester to Minster did, however, provide us with some interesting experiences. With apologies to Madeleine, one issue that arose when making the long drive, was that after half an hour or so Madeleine started to complain of feeling carsick. We gave her ginger biscuits to eat, because ginger had been an old remedy for sea and travel sickness, and it does work. On one journey, Margaret handed Madeleine a packet of ginger biscuits. After about 30/40 minutes, a voice from the back asked, 'Mummy, can I stop eating the biscuits now?'

Madeleine and Lissie would on the odd occasion get very irritable with each other on these journeys, and Lissie recently reminded me how Madeleine would sometimes bring up some 'green gunge' to taunt her with. I can also recall threatening to stop the car on a few occasions and throw both of them out onto the motorway if they did not stop winding each other up. But on the whole, given the long journeys, they were astonishingly patient and well behaved. With the shorter journeys, we had no problems.

During this initial period in the hospital flat, my mother was allowed to stay with us for a week, primarily I think to give her a rest. It went very well, but on the drive back to Minster, she alarmed me by suddenly undoing her seat belt and making to open the car door. I think all she wanted to do was take off her cardigan but forgot where she was. This was a clear early indication of her eventual decline.

Eventually we sold our Manchester house, so in July 1982 we were able to move in to our newly-bought house in the village of Loose, on the outskirts of Maidstone, The house dated from around 1820 and needed constant attention. But it suited us, and we loved it, having as it did a very large garden. Having moved to Loose, both children then transferred to the nearby junior school. It was situated almost behind our house, and we could hear the children during play breaks. The headmaster took a shine to both girls.

Locally, Loose suffered all manner of jokes, such as the Loose Bowls Club having its noticeboard overwritten as the 'Loose bowels club'. The cartoonist Ralph Steadman, who lived in the village, designed the calendar for 1989. He included a photo of this 'Loose Bowels Club' and another of the 'Loose Women Morris Dancers', along with other photos depicting the local postmaster's shop with the comment 'girlie mags' and rubber balls' (true!), and one of the local policeman on his cycle travelling down the steep Loose Hill but with the photo reversed, thus depicting him as cycling on the wrong side of the road. The Post Office objected, and refused to sell the calendar (but did not stop selling 'girlie mags' and rubber balls)! The local policeman was also very offended, but I do not recall him refusing to police the village.

Both children then went to secondary school, with Madeleine going to Oldborough Manor School and then, having passed the ridiculous and divisive '13 plus', went to the Invicta Grammar School. Lissie went first to Cornwallis School, then passed the '13 plus' but left behind her best friend, who did not take kindly to Lissie's success. Eventually, it appeared that Lissie was not thriving, so we took her out – to the dismay of the head teacher who said he wanted to keep children like ours to enhance the school's reputation.

The headmaster had been a fairly new appointment but had refused to move house, because he wanted to continue to live in Surrey where his children could continue to go to their local comprehensive school. Surrey had moved to the comprehensive system years earlier, while Kent stubbornly refused to give up its out-dated grammar school system with entry after a '13 plus' exam. This meant that so many children who had made friends were split up at that late age if they were not all successful in the exam. Later, the Authority saw limited sense and changed to the better '11 plus' exam, which led to far fewer upsets amongst friends. Since there is evidence that Kent has voted Conservative since the Norman Invasion, to get Kent to abandon the grammar school system, still in existence (as I write in 2021), would need a similar invasion/revolution.

We enrolled Lissie in Kent College, a private Quaker foundation school in Pembury, near Tunbridge Wells, where she did extremely well. It entailed me driving her to school, which was fine, but to this day she apparently recalls an incident that has imprinted itself into her brain. One freezing morning, with snow and ice on most of the route to Pembury, I must have relaxed just a fraction on the very stretch of road that was the most heavily iced, and I skidded. The car ended up facing the opposite direction. No big deal. I carried on as if nothing had happened, but Lissie has a clear memory, etched forever in a mythical past.

When I arrived in October 1981, the Maidstone District Health Authority was one of five districts managed within the Kent Area Health Authority. This was one of the arcane management variations in just a few areas in the otherwise sensible arrangements that had been introduced in 1972. It meant that Maidstone had its own district management, but under the overall management of the Kent Area Authority. This was over-complicated and recognised as such when these multi-district Area Health Authorities were abolished in 1984. Thus Maidstone Health Authority became an independent authority.

Soon after I took up this post, and given the reason for leaving Prestwich/Salford with the inevitable self-doubts after that bruising experience, I have to admit being delighted with one personal achievement. I had applied to the British Psychological Society to be elected a 'Fellow' of the Society. At that time just 4-5% of the membership of the British Psychological Society were Fellows. (At the time of writing, it is down to 2%). I was duly elected. For me, this felt like a full endorsement by the British Psychological Society of all my efforts in Prestwich/Salford, which I knew the Society was well aware of. However, I fully recognise that the support and hard work of all my psychology colleagues in Prestwich/Salford contributed enormously. Without their hard work and dedication, nothing could have been achieved. I doubt if any of them will ever read this, but if they do, my heartfelt thanks to all of them.

The department I took over, namely Maidstone D.H.A. Psychology Department, was housed within the grounds of Barming

Mental Hospital – an adult psychiatric establishment. Barming Hospital was one of the very first large psychiatric establishments in the UK, some say the very first. A local story, true or just myth, was that the name of the hospital led to the popular term 'barmy'.

The department consisted of three psychologists and a secretary, all housed within the end of an adult psychiatric ward, though the connection between the two had been blocked. There were two other cabins, one of which was my office. It was very comfortable.

My first task was to find out what each psychologist was doing, and I found that all three only saw adult mental health outpatients, with referrals from psychiatrists and GPs. Their service had a very high and well-deserved reputation.

The problem was that the previous department heads had never developed service to other specialisms where psychologists were already proving their worth elsewhere, such as in services to children and their families, or to geriatric, psycho-psychiatric, learning difficulties, long-stay rehabilitation, paediatrics, or forensic services. All these had to be developed but needed finance for new posts.

In an effort to make any new senior post more attractive in an era when psychologists were not plentiful, I made contact with the Psychology Department at the University of Kent at Canterbury, so that new applicants or any of the existing staff that had the inclination could establish research projects in association with the university. In the event, this was never taken up.

I learned that two of the psychologists were each providing a weekly session within the boundaries of another health authority, namely Tunbridge Wells. I was told this was historical, but the Maidstone management appeared to know nothing about it! Fortunately, the NHS reorganisation that abolished the system of multi-District Area Health Authorities, made these arrangements obsolete, as Maidstone became its own stand-alone authority. I immediately stopped my staff from providing their weekly service to our neighbour. I was told some psychiatrists serving this neighbour complained, but not to me. However, the deed was done.

Because of the gaps in Maidstone's service, I decided to see the various consultants in charge of these services to explore expansion. That was my job and why I had been appointed. Funding for the new forensic unit was taken out of 'storage', advertised, and filled.

To develop other new posts, the first person I saw was the Consultant Child Psychiatrist, who had a small medical team housed close to Maidstone town centre. We met for lunch to discuss whether he wanted psychology to be part of his outfit, as was the practice in most health authorities, but it was difficult to keep him to the topic as he kept on talking about his children and two injured fingers he had recently had heavily bandaged. In the end, I managed to get a promise that he would consult with his two colleagues and get back to me. This was in October 1981. As I write this (spring and summer of 2021), I am still waiting for him to get back to me! I started a service myself.

Starting this child service had its problems. I felt that as the psychology department was based within the grounds of an adult psychiatric hospital, I could not ask parents to bring their children to these grounds, nor to travel from all the outlying villages – some of which were around 20 miles' distance.

In addition, most families who were likely to be referred depended on public transport and would have had to travel by bus into the centre of town, then take a change of bus to the hospital, and then similar intolerable return journeys.

Therefore, I decided to base the child service entirely on home visiting. Some of the few older adolescents who were referred wanted to be seen away from their home, so they were seen in my office. But later on, the department was given its own premises just off the main hospital site, which made it acceptable.

While this decision to see children in their own homes was initially taken on purely practical grounds, in the event I found that it had enormous benefits and completely altered my view of how children's services should be provided. It enabled me to see how the family interacted with each other within a home where they were comfortable, and therefore gave a much clearer idea of the problem than any attempt by the parent to explain to the

GP and the GP's précis of the parent's understanding conveyed in their referral letter to the psychologist. This allowed me to observe 'the problem' first hand within the family home and with a parent present. This was a significant contrast to many children's treatment units, where often only the child is seen without a parent. Or if a parent is seen, it is in a totally alien environment.

The practice in so many children's treatment facilities, where so often only the child is seen, is in my view a classic example of an interpretation of the 'medical' model, where the problem is located 'within the child'. It's as if the problem is an 'illness', therefore there is no need to speak to a parent, or inform the parent of what, if anything, they themselves could do to help or alter family practices. Pills will do the trick.

It has to be said that the above practice is by no means universal within child centres, but they do exist. And many psychologists appear to follow this model, whether willingly or not. Psychology living in the Dark Ages, ignoring hundreds of psychology research articles and textbooks within the field of child development, which constantly show the influence of parenting. I suspect that where psychologists working within children's units want to involve the parents, the medical model is too strong for them to alter the practice. Seeing children with their parents in their own home sheds a completely different perspective on the problem, matching up with decades of research into child development. Let me make it absolutely clear, though. Seeing children and a parent does not mean a parent is 'to blame'. It simply recognises that children grow up with their parents.

So, I started a service to children, but seeing all of them with at least one parent and within their own home. Judging by the feedback and volume of referrals over the following years, I have good reasons to believe that all the various referrers, from General Practitioners, Community Paediatricians, Social Workers, and Health Visitors, found this approach to have been very helpful.

Within the next few years I achieved funding for three Principal Psychology posts – one within Psychiatric Rehabilitation, one within the Elderly, and one within Learning Difficulties – a senior post for the Elderly, and some years later, after a further management reorganisation, two new senior posts within the child specialty.

There were no particular problems, at least none worth recording. The psychiatrists serving the adult population left us alone, though I always attended the monthly Professional Management Meetings, along with all the senior staff. The GPs were satisfied, and we were able to continue providing an already existing service within two GP practices.

In saying the psychiatrists left us alone, I can recall one incident when I seriously upset one psychiatrist. He had asked me to see one of his in-patients. This was a young man who had been responsible for an arson incident and, as a consequence, had been admitted to the hospital. When I saw him on his ward, he appeared outwardly perfectly sane and in control of himself, but complained bitterly that he had been illegally placed within a locked ward. He was correct. To be admitted to hospital and then to be locked up without the individual's consent required the full procedure required by the Mental Health Act. He had not been detained under the provisions of the Mental Health Act and so was bitterly resentful as a result. I was essentially asked to treat him for his 'unreasonable' anger and resentment, which the psychiatrist felt was hindering his treatment. But he was in no mood for treatment. I said I could not treat him unless the legality of his incarceration was sorted out. The psychiatrist was furious and, I presume, seriously embarrassed. During one committee meeting, he accused me of being unhelpful. He never referred anyone else to me again! I did not brood.

It seemed I arrived with a bit of a reputation among some of the senior psychologists elsewhere in the region, and so I was asked to chair the local branch of the BPS Clinical Division and later asked to take on the organisation of the annual Post Qualification Regional Training Weeks for the SE Thames Region psychologists for a three-year stint. The region consisted of Kent, Surrey, East Sussex, and South London. However, among one or two local senior psychologists, it seems my presence was not altogether welcomed. I suspect they felt their own position in the region's hierarchy had been displaced. This was nonsense, as far as I was concerned, but it did have ramifications for Margaret.

Having moved south, she did not want to remain idle, and therefore she was faced with the decision of how to proceed in the job market. There were two options. She saw an advert for a position within the Government Employment Advice Offices, went for the interview, and was successful. We discussed this a lot, but a problem was that such government departments were then under scrutiny in the era of 'Thatcher cuts', so her future would always be in doubt.

Another option was to apply to the local Clinical Psychology Regional Training Scheme. It was always clear to me that the psychologist in charge of the appointment process at that time was hostile to (jealous of?) me! So we discussed whether she should apply under her married name, or give her maiden name. Somehow, we arrived at the decision to apply under her married name, and she failed to get appointed! This led to her becoming a Health Visitor. We will never know if she would have been appointed to the clinical course if she had applied under her maiden name, but I never had any doubt that she would have made an excellent clinical psychologist. Another 'what if', but she then embarked upon a very successful career as a Health Visitor.

Being by this time very senior within the Clinical Psychology world, I was frequently asked to be an external assessor on appointment panels for Head of Department appointments around the NHS. I also sat on appeal panels as a Psychology Trade Union representative for psychologists appealing against all sorts of problems within their own authorities. This was all good fun but often entailed long journeys and overnight stays, leaving Margaret alone with the children. A problem with such roles is that one rarely gets feedback as to whether one's recommendations turned into successful appointments/achievements.

In 1983, I spent three weeks up in Cumbria as part of a team appointed by the Hospital Advisory Authority. This authority had been set up many years earlier as an attempt to improve the standard of all psychiatric hospitals after the many scandals and public enquiries. We inspected the local psychiatric hospital, and my job was to examine the Psychology Department. To say it was lacking is somewhat of an understatement! It was not just backward; rather, it was doing things that well-meaning hospital visitors would do, like teaching patients card games or 'pass the parcel'.

Much later in 1987/8, the same organisation, namely the Hospital Advisory Committee, inspected the Maidstone Health Authority Mental Health Services, including my Psychology Department. I asked every psychologist to write up an account of their activities within their various specialties, and I wrote up a history of the department since I had arrived.

The report that came back said, 'All aspects of the psychology department are examples of good practice.' The authority's Medical Officer, Dr Bussey, met me after this report at some reception and called the Psychology Department 'the jewel in the crown'. Over the many years that I had been reading these reports on other psychiatric hospitals, I had never come across such an accolade! Congratulations to all my hard-working colleagues. It was their achievement. But I have to admit that I did give myself a pat on the back!

In the early 1980s, the Government reformed the Mental Health Act, which had been in existence for many years but needed updating. The purpose of the Act was to safeguard patients who were admitted to hospital under a 'detention order' against their will, in order to protect them and to protect the public. The new act, published in 1983, legislated for the setting up of the Mental Health Act Commission – a body consisting of approximately 80 members. Their job was to visit every psychiatric establishment at regular intervals, to review the arrangements, treatment, and care of such 'detained' patients. A multi-disciplinary group of professionals were then appointed to carry out this task.

The Commission consisted of various professions. There were approximately 20 psychiatrists, ten lawyers, ten psychiatric nurses, ten clinical psychologists, ten social workers, and about ten laypersons, plus a few GPs and occupational therapists. I am not sure just how the other professionals came to be appointed, but the Department of Health asked the British Psychological

Society to nominate psychologists. This request was passed down to our regional psychology group and I was asked if I would like to be nominated. I did not need to hesitate. I said yes! I had no great expectations as to how such a body would work, but also no illusions about whether or not some psychiatrists would want to dominate the proceedings. In the event, some certainly did want to dominate.

The overall chairperson was a Conservative Politician, Lord Colville, who turned out to a brilliant chairman, probably the best I had ever had the privilege of witnessing. The Commission was organised into three groupings – one for the South, one for the Midlands, and one for the North – with each group tasked with inspecting all the psychiatric establishments within their area that housed detained patients. Another local Conservative politician, Mrs Gillian Shepherd, who had been a local councillor in Norfolk and then chair of that authority, chaired the Southern grouping. Later, she became an MP, and for the last few years of the John Major government was the Education Secretary.

Gillian Shepherd rivalled Lord Colville's brilliance as a chairperson. Both had the ability, among many others, of keeping noisy individual members – mainly a few psychiatrists – from taking over and dominating, but they did it with such subtlety that it was hardly noticed. This led to the Commission becoming a genuine and functional multi-professional body.

Each of the three regional groups was then further subdivided into smaller visiting teams. These small teams had the task of carrying weekly whole-day visits to the various psychiatric establishments, as well as attending regular regional meetings in London.

The lawyer on the group I attended was Michael Edward-Evans, who lived in a huge house next door to the home of Charles Darwin! He was a major influence in our group and of immense support. Later, he agreed to have Madeleine do work experience within his firm.

Sadly, after the first four-year term of the chairman, Lord Colville retired. The next four years saw another chairman take up post. He was quite an eminent barrister who had clearly become used to dealing with 'medical experts' in the courts. However, as Commission chairman he would continue to defer to medical opinion and ignore any other professional opinion if there was a divergence of views. This slowly began to disrupt the previous excellent multi-disciplinary co-operation. At an annual meeting, this became more and more apparent.

As a result, I volunteered to speak to the issue before the entire Commission. I prepared a speech, after which there was a vote. I lost, but only by about two or three votes out of a total of over 80. Nearly all the psychiatrists and psychiatric nurses voted in favour of the chairman! I am not sure how many pounds in weight I lost as a result of all the tension involved, but I later received the warmest congratulations from a very senior and respected member of the Commission and an elder statesman within Clinical Psychology, who was present at the meeting.

I do not think my intervention led to any change in the conduct of this chairman. He was in all likelihood too set in his ways to recognise his bias, but I never regretted my attempt to steer the way the Commission worked back to the successful first model.

Each appointment to the Commission was for 4 years, but at the end of this period around half were reappointed. I was one of those reappointed. Most of the hospitals we visited appeared to take these visits seriously, except for Broadmoor Hospital, which was still living in the Dark Ages. Awful. We learned at the time that a lay visitor was a certain Jimmy Saville, of later ill fame and infamous child abuse. The hospital denied knowing, but this always appeared implausible.

Another hospital for the elderly that we visited also had its attitude problems. On the ward that looked after the oldest patients, they were arranged up against the wall with nothing to do. (Had they adopted this First World War practice from Prestwich?) When confronted, the Charge Nurse commented that it was OK as they were 'all waiting to die'. The other members of the team could not believe what they had heard. This was their first encounter with such an out-dated opinion.

In another very large and private care home, but with some Local Authority-paid beds, there was a wing that was very lavishly furnished, with the elderly in spacious accommodation often with a sitting room and bedroom. The rooms were all immaculately kept. In another part of the home, where the local authority paid for the elderly, the rooms were standard Local Authority-type accommodation. It stank. Pitiful.

Another task of the Commission was to establish a group of members who were specifically assigned to visit patients who were due to receive neuro-surgery. This was painful for me, as only the psychiatrist on the group had the right to approve or not approve the actual surgery, and was therefore the only one in the team who could delve into their respective problems. But, of course, this was from a strictly psychiatric point of view. The other members of the visiting team had only to ensure the patient was being adequately looked after. The psychiatrist in my group invariably approved this very invasive procedure. I frequently felt that such surgery was inappropriate, because what the patients needed, but had never received, was appropriate psychological therapy that could have avoided the need for surgery. I had to keep my mouth shut.

I must relate another experience when visiting a private hospital in the Midlands. This hospital was outside the normal visiting area of my group, but on this occasion the Midlands team was unable to get their team together.

This visit proved to be an occasion where a person's reputation – accurate or not – preceded him. The hospital had established a psychologically-based regime on one adolescent ward, referred to as a 'Token Economy Ward'. This regime followed basic principles of learning that applied to all individuals. All good parenting and teaching follow these principles, even when the parent/teacher is unaware of it. When applied within a hospital ward, the same principles are used, but in such cases it is the job of the staff to undo the problems that led to institutionalisation in the first place – as mentioned previously when discussing Prestwich Hospital- or in this case, teaching positive behaviour for youngsters who had had unfortunate and inadequate home upbringings. This establishment and ward had in fact been visited years earlier by some of the Prestwich psychologists when they had been far from impressed.

When I visited this ward, I was met by what appeared to be a fairly junior nurse who had been assigned to meet me. After some preliminaries, during which he said he understood what the ward was about, I asked him what behaviour of the youngsters they reinforced. He replied that if they did 'so and so' (I have forgotten the actual example of this and other replies) the person would get punished! So I asked again. He then gave me another example of some behaviour and how he and his colleagues responded – namely with another punishment. The same response came a third and fourth time. I asked a fifth time, and the penny dropped. He understood that he and his colleagues should have chosen some behaviour that was appropriate for the young person and rewarded it! He was very embarrassed and mortified and hardly knew where to look.

However, I persisted in asking what happened if, in their eyes, a youngster behaved very badly. The answer was simple: they locked him up! When I pointed out the young inhabitants of this ward were already locked up, he replied that there was a space within the ward where they locked up such miscreants, which I presumed to be a small side ward. So I asked how soon was it after any misdemeanour before they were (further) locked up, and the reply was, 'Immediately.' Then, how many such misdemeanours were required to get locked up? Just 'one' was the reply. I then asked the obvious, namely what did they have to do to get out? 'Be good,' came the reply. 'How soon after they were "good" would they be let out?' They had to be 'good' for at least one week, came the reply. What a mis-match! Dreadful.

At the end of each such visit, each visiting team reported their findings to the Managers (the members of the Hospital Management Board). So we duly settled down for the end-of-visit report and waited for the hospital staff to arrive. They duly did, including a man I identified as a psychiatrist, sitting himself next to a woman I had identified as a psychologist. I overheard the psychiatrist ask the psychologist, 'Who is that chap?', looking at me! She told him, and I heard him exclaim, 'Oh, bloody hell.'

Make of this what you will, but I took it as a compliment. I hope I lived up to this reputation by lambasting the hospital for their pretend psychologically-based ward programme. It was dreadful. It totally failed to understand the basic psychological principals they should have been following, namely reinforcing behaviour that was progressive by positive reinforcement instead of teaching them purely what not to do. I also pointed out that the only way any person in a psychiatric hospital should be locked up within the law was by implementing the provisions of the Mental Health Act, which had in fact been carried out for around half of the youngsters within this ward. But I pointed out that the other half were also locked up but without any implementation of the Mental Health provisions, therefore locked up illegally. We told the 'Managers' to sort out this problem. I have no idea if they did, and if they did, how they did it. But I hope I lived up to whatever reputation I had in the eyes of the psychiatrist mentioned above.

Looking back at this involvement with the Mental Health Commission, I only really recognised later that the effort of combining this Commission work with my Health Authority work was distracting me from the latter, and slowly leading me to 'taking my eye off the ball'. I am sure the psychology staff became rather disgruntled, though none ever said so. This would have been totally justifiable.

In addition, throughout my time there, or anywhere else, I had just one disciplinary problem. This was quite early after I arrived in Maidstone, and it involved just one member of my staff. The problem was minor in itself, but if not checked could have become a substantial issue of fraud, and therefore had to be dealt with. I suspect I could have handled it better than I did, because it did become rather messy and lead to tension within the department for quite a while.

Another serious domestic downside was that I often had to leave home in the very early morning and come back late, leaving Margaret, who had her own difficult job, and Madeleine and Lissie. I am not sure how she coped, but she did, and never with a single complaint.

Back to the everyday NHS. A problem we all had to deal with was NHS reorganisation. The first major reorganisation following the establishment of the NHS occurred in 1974 (mentioned above), that placed all previously independent hospitals into a combined authority that managed all hospitals within their Local Authority boundary. This was tweaked in 1984. But now, from mid-1980s, there was an endless succession of NHS reorganisation. As soon as one established good relationships with colleagues on various planning committees, there was a change in the organisation and all planning had to start again. One example was that within a Paediatric Planning Group I attended, I quickly obtained the agreement that there should be a Principal Psychologist post to head up the Child Psychology specialty. At the first such meeting I attended, this post was put into the plans but as the fourth post down the list to be financed. By the next meeting, it moved up to second place, so I was quite confident that at the next meeting it would be top of the list. We then suffered another reorganisation – the planning group was disbanded – with nothing put in its place except for one individual GP who took all decisions on his own. The result? No new psychology post!

Another management re-organisation meant new appointments at the very senior management level, thus getting rid of Hospital Secretaries, who ran the place together with a group of senior medical and other staff, and inaugurated the era of the 'Chief Executive'. There was one period in the late 1980s when the Government had the idea that retired Generals, Admirals, Air Marshals, or even lowly Colonels would make the best Chief Executives. It was a disaster. I think it is true that not a single such appointment lasted for more than a year, as the job proved to be completely beyond their experience and their competence. Managing an Army unit or naval ship proved to be easy in comparison, and left them totally ill-equipped to deal with the complexities of the NHS. Maidstone escaped such an appointment, putting an experienced medical administrator in post – a decent and competent man. However, after a few years in the post, he was told one evening by the Chairman of the Authority to clear his desk and be gone by the next morning. Nobody ever saw him again. Just outrageous.

Yet another national reorganisation split up unified departments such as psychology, and put every psychologist and other professionals working within a defined specialty into small multi-professional management units, with its own leader. This meant the end of unified professional departments and destroyed the unity of such departments as psychology, with its psychologist head, answerable only to the Hospital Secretary/later Chief Executive. When the head psychologist was in charge, it meant, for example, that the Hospital Chief Executive could not interfere with the purely professional running of the department or how psychologists interpreted their role. Now, any professional could be appointed to run a small multi-disciplinary unit, whether or not that person knew anything of the role or job of the other professions within that unit! A backward step to a prehistoric era, which the provisions and recommendations within the Trethowan Report, implemented by the NHS Principles Committee (mentioned earlier) and its recommendations mentioned above attempted successfully to rectify, only to be undone 15 years later.

This last reorganisation in 1989/90 also divided the Psychiatric Unit from the General Medical Unit. Thus, the Psychiatric Unit was a step back to the day prior to 1974 when psychiatric hospitals became stand-alone hospitals. Was this a far-seeing and progressive forward-looking, or backward-looking step? Others can decide. I know how I felt.

There have been endless complaints about the management of the NHS for as long as I can recall. But how can any organisation work efficiently when it is constantly being re-organised at the whim of some Conservative Government politician. (With one exception – a Labour Minister of Health, and that was to undo an earlier re-organisation.) Looking back, it seemed that Conservative Government meddling was all in the slow direction of privatisation – first, in small instalments; and from 2010, in ever-increasing speed.

However, a minor plus that followed this reorganisation meant that I was moved to the General Hospital, but still in charge of the Child Specialty. I was given the funds to appoint two Senior Psychologists and Secretary to work solely within the Child

Specialty, and this worked out very well. We did what needed to be done and were never interfered with by the professional hierarchy above me and by the various staff I was nominally responsible to. It is possible they never knew what I was doing. I never told them.

After five years, there was yet another NHS reorganisation, which put me back into the group I had left five years earlier! Worse still was that I had little respect for the new Chief Executive – a psychiatric nurse who thought he knew everything there was to know about anything. I had known him since shortly after I arrived in Maidstone and had had some dealings with him, which always left me singularly unimpressed. So now he was to be my boss. I met him and said I really did not want to work in his unit, and I was sure he did not want to manage me, so asked if he would he think of making me an offer I could not refuse, and I would then take early retirement from the NHS. To his credit, he did just that and offered me a redundancy package that was the maximum allowed within the NHS. I jumped at it and retired on a very substantial package. I had no regrets. I doubt if he had any regrets either, though I knew he had used up his entire budget for such purposes.

I knew from feedback from medical staff, and in particular two Consultant Community Paediatricians, GPs, and Social Services, that our service was highly respected. So I felt justified in retiring from full-time NHS work on a high, with my work well done.

Margaret also retired a year or so after I did, due to increasing difficulty she had with her hearing, so finding it difficult to do her job as a health visitor. So there we were, just two old aged pensioners, but not yet old enough to receive the State Pension.

CHAPTER 11

Following retirement

While I was more than ready to leave the ever-increasing NHS politics and endless re-organisations, none of which (apart from abolishing multi-district authorities) was to my mind an improvement on the last, I was far from ready to stop working as a psychologist.

I set about arranging other avenues of work and negotiated sessions at the Maidstone Private Hospital and also at another private hospital in Medway. Initially, I used my old contacts with psychiatrists and GPs to obtain referrals, which they provided in large numbers. Most individuals referred having private health insurance, which I found much more comfortable to deal with in contrast to individuals who paid for themselves.

I also managed to negotiate sessional work within two GP practices, one in Snodland, Kent, which had been a heavy referrer to my department while still in the NHS, and the other in Walderslade, Medway. The GP practices had by then been given their own budgets to employ whoever they wanted, and this was the arrangement that enabled them to hire me. I did this for five years, initially one half-day session per week each, but by the last year I was doing two half-day sessions a week in Snodland and three half-day sessions a week in Walderslade. It helped to pay the mortgage! This arrangement came to an end some time in the year 2000 after yet another NHS reorganisation that ended the arrangement whereby general practices were given their own budgets to spend as they wished. The consequence was that my sessions, arranged with and funded by the two practices, had to end.

Psychology for both the two GP surgeries where I worked now came under the control of the Medway Psychology Dept.

The new Head saw me and asked if I wished to continue. She explained that she would be pleased to have me on board, but that I would have to comply with her decision of seeing individuals for eight sessions only, unless I was authorised by her to do more. I knew these arrangements had been creeping into some psychology departments, under direction from dumb senior managers, but it was a system that I had never implemented nor would ever have contemplated implementing had I remained in charge of a department. Imagine telling a surgeon that a specific operation had to be done within a certain time, and if this was not possible in any particular case, to gain permission from a manager before the operation could be completed. How long would it take before it was realised the operation needed more time? Would the operating team just stop until permission came? Bizarre. I told the new Head of Psychology just what I thought, ever so politely, and ended my arrangements with both GP practices.

An additional weekly therapy session at 10 Harley Street, London, had been arranged as soon as I retired in 1995. I had to present myself to be vetted by the manager, to see if I was suitable for what they thought was a very prestigious address (!), and I was judged to be suitable and passed their scrutiny. I hired one room for one evening session a week, which also enabled me to inspect local shops, museums, and restaurants. I carried on these sessions when I left Maidstone for Portishead, until I finally retired and stopped all work in 2013.

After I retired from NHS employment, alongside the work at the two GP practices, I also started providing legal reports, which started in the area of personal injury, mostly following road traffic accidents, and accidents at work, plus a few medical negligence cases. An ever-increasing number of referrals involved Family Law cases and a few in the area of Criminal Law.

I practised in these areas of individual and Family Law work until I finally retired in 2013. Initially, referrals came via the first secretary I had been given when I moved to the general hospital in Maidstone, who had set up her own agency which obtained referrals from solicitors. After this had developed, referrals increasingly came directly to me, but this meant I had to do all my own typing of the reports! Hard work, but it did enable me to come to terms with computers.

At some point shortly after I retired from the NHS, I found myself recruited onto the board of the local 'Maidstone Home Start' Committee. Many local Home Start groups existed all over the country, set up to assist mothers with their young children by involving other mothers in mentoring them and giving mothering advice within their clients' own homes. Margaret had been involved and been on the committee before my involvement. My own participation was only in attending regular committee meetings and the annual get-together for all volunteer home workers.

At one such annual meeting, there where many new volunteers. So each committee member was asked to introduce him/herself by giving a brief two or three-minute talk about themselves, their area of work, etc. When it was my turn, I got up and thought I had better explain why I was visibly soaking wet all down my right-hand side. I explained that as I had driven into the car park, the heavens opened with a ferocious rainstorm. So I'd remained seated in the car for a while, waiting for the downpour to ease up. While waiting, I noticed an apparition approaching along the pavement – a young lady walking through this downpour, no umbrella, stark naked... apart from her shoes.

I explained that by pure coincidence, I had felt it was time to get out of the car just as this apparition approached alongside. I opened my door and the rain poured into the car as I paused for a second or so (just to make sure I was seeing what I was seeing – which was only proper), then I did get out and opened my umbrella, which the wind promptly blew out! Hence my soaking! For some perverse and unaccountable reason, this caused the entire meeting to collapse into a bout of uncontrollable laughter. I had been due to take over the chairmanship for the next year, but we moved house before I could do so.

Another organisation I had been invited to join was a local Kent-based group that vetted prospective foster carers. The job of the group was to examine their background and judge if we thought they were suitable. This was always an odd remit, as we never saw the candidates, who had been separately previously checked out by social workers, so we merely had to judge candidates on the basis of the social worker's report. My first committee meeting was held in a school in Broadstairs, just a few weeks after I had bought my first Mercedes in 1997. I arrived, parked the car, and a young lad came out of a door and slung a pebble in my direction. It missed me but hit the car, leaving a chip! On my brand-new car! Fortunately, a teacher had witnessed this 'outrageous' behaviour and the school paid for repairs.

After our very wet, abandoned holiday that I mentioned previously while we were still living in Manchester, we had bought a trailer tent which was much more convenient. We used this for the first three holidays after we moved to Maidstone, but then camping began to lose its appeal for Margaret. Instead of camping, we went to France for the next three holidays, but staying in gites instead. By then we had bought cycles for us all and took them with us, enjoying some lovely memorable long bike rides. Our first holiday took us to the countryside just to the northeast of Montargis. One of our cycle excursions was about 60K each way, from Montargis to Fontainebleau and back. Madeleine and Lissie were introduced to their very first Michelin-starred restaurant, Le Gamin. They thought they had gone to heaven.

We were recommended another very good restaurant nearby in a farmhouse. There was no choice – and no menu. We would be given whatever the cook had available. We were sure Lissie would not like what was offered, which turned out to be rabbit, so we pretended it was from some other animal. But she was not fooled!

Our next holiday was in the Loire region, near Saumur, and our last about 60 miles southeast of Bordeaux. All were very memorable holidays. I think it was the following year that Margaret and myself went to the Auvergne region for a holiday, and it was here that we experienced our first three-star Michelin restaurant, namely Michel Bras, situated in the middle of mountains and forests near the town of Laguiole. We stayed overnight in their very new hotel, and the food was superb. An irritating problem occurred at a nearby table where an expensive looking gentleman was dining together with a much younger looking partner, and each and every course led to him complaining.

The waiters were astonishingly polite, but this man did not get any dish replaced.

My 60th birthday was particularly memorable. Margaret had booked a long weekend stay in Paris, which I knew about. But she had not told me that she had booked a return trip on Concorde. It was an amazing surprise and experience, going to Paris on the new Eurotunnel train, and flying back over the English Channel towards Cornwall, then back up the Bristol Channel and so back to Heathrow. Concorde flew so high that the English Channel looked like a small river. The trip was late afternoon, and halfway through the trip the pilot suggested we look out of the windows to observe the plane catching up with the sunset. Surreal. It was a very lovely present.

After we moved to Maidstone, we always visited my mother a few times a year, and gradually more and more frequently as she deteriorated. She had stayed with us again for a week around 1995/6, and I took the opportunity of driving past the house in Woldingham where we'd lived in the last years of the war. The house was much as it was – with a small extension to the front – but still very visible was the 'tall' two-feet high straggly hedge that my sister Maria and myself ducked behind as we contemplated obliteration by the V2 rocket.

Over the last year or so, I doubt if my mother really knew much about her environment. On one visit near the end, she suddenly said, 'What shall we do with the children?' Both Margaret and I felt that she was talking to my father, probably some time during the war, or perhaps while they were still in Vienna.

She continued to deteriorate until she died in 1997, which would in all likelihood have occurred two to three years earlier had it not been for the devoted attention and skilled nursing she received within Minster Abbey. Both Margaret and I had observed the extraordinary devotion and care she had been given by Sister Patricia – a nun who had joined the community at the same time as my mother. She had been a nurse in Ireland before joining the Minster community, and looked after my mother in a way she would never have been looked after had she been cared for in a local authority care home.

My mother's funeral was a time of rejoicing for the nuns. An aspect of death in a religious community is, of course, that it is a wonderful occasion. Due to their strong religious beliefs, they 'know' that the deceased will go immediately to heaven! For the rest of us, mainly her family, it was difficult – as any funeral usually is.

Many years later, in 2019, we visited the convent on our way to France, primarily to visit Sister Patricia, who we knew had been ill for some time. We were actually surprised she had lived for so long after she first became ill, and were expecting to see someone barely conscious. But no. We were taken up to her room and found her sitting up in bed as happy as anyone could possibly be. She knew she was about to go to heaven, so death was wonderful; for her and the rest of the community, it was the fulfilment of their whole lives. We heard she died just a week or so after we visited.

While all this was happening, we saw Madeleine going to West London University to study for a Law degree, and then Lissie went to Cardiff University for a Teaching degree. When Madeleine finished, she did a Postgraduate course in Bristol, while Lissie completed her teacher training degree course in Cardiff.

Soon after she moved into her first 'digs', Madeleine had the unfortunate experience of being burgled. On another occasion when she was ill, I went to collect her. On the journey home, she felt sick, so while still on the motorway I opened the window and suggested she stick her head out if she felt she was about to be sick. She *was* sick, and she did stick her head out of the window, but not quite far enough. The rear of the car experienced just what 'sick' was like!

Before Lissie had left to go to Cardiff, we had observed just how very difficult it was for her to keep her room in some semblance of order. After she had gone to university, we cleared out her room and her clothes cupboard and found a very old, decayed, non- smelly lump of cat poo! At home, Lissie had the smaller of the three bedrooms, and it was really too small to contain all her clothes and clobber. But when we visited her in her university residence, her room was immaculate!

At home, it had sometimes been an effort for Lissie to get up and organised in the mornings. But we learned that she was now the one in her Hall of Residence block who organised all the other students and made sure they all got up etc.! Moral: Never judge a daughter based on what they do at home, or something like that.

Lissie had to contend with two bizarre episodes. She, like all teacher trainees, had to spend time in a classroom, and thus gain real life experience in schools. One such school was in Aberfan. This was the Welsh Valley village that experienced the horrific accident in 1966, when a huge coal tip collapsed onto the local infant and junior school, killing 116 children and 28 staff. A visit to the local cemetery where all the victims are buried is chilling, moving, and very disturbing. All these years later, the local headmaster only ever spoke to Lissie via another teacher. He would never talk to her directly. Such, presumably, was his animosity to the English! Disgraceful, but on reflection perhaps not all that surprising, given that the coal tip disaster, which Dr. Robens – the head of the Coal Board at the time, and who had been a Labour Government Minister – refused to apologise for. The accident had resulted from neglect over very many years.

Lissie's next trauma was in her next school. At first, she got on well with the class teacher, but after a while nothing she did was deemed to be acceptable by the woman. I recall a long telephone conversation with Lissie, who seemed to me to be on the point of giving up. I tried to reassure her, as it seemed to me that the teacher was jealous of her rather than being genuinely critical. To give Lissie her due, and to her everlasting credit, she persevered and got through her ordeal.

One of the pleasures of our house in Maidstone was the large garden. It was hard work keeping it in order, but it supplied us with our own dessert and cooking apples, raspberries, and black and redcurrants, Victoria plums, greengages, and Jerusalem artichokes. It was hard work and there were far too many apples for us to eat, or for Margaret to cook. These were all well established when we bought the house, and Margaret then established a thriving herb garden.

One of the apple trees was an old one that had been allowed to grow into a very large, full-size tree at the back of the garden. It produced a massive amount of cooking apples, which took ages of backbreaking effort to pick. This could only be done after the apples had fallen, as the tree was too large to be able to take them directly off the tree. Fortunately, or not, the massive storm experienced in the south of England of 1987 tore the tree down.

That great storm of 1987 saw me away in Yorkshire, acting as one of a number of tutors on a Health Visitors' annual refresher course. The course went well, and I think I was able to contribute a bit. One amusing experience was how I was treated during one evening meal. The tutors all sat together, and opposite me sat a female tutor. Not only would she not speak to me, but if she found she had to change her gaze after speaking to a female staff member opposite and to my left, I noticed that she would change her gaze but circle her eyes over and above me and then down again, before settling down to speak to the other female on my right! She had clearly not come to terms with herself. Weird. Or was I just not good-looking enough? Or too good-looking?

But back to the great storm of 1987. I was absent during the storm as I was involved with the above Health Visitors' annual refresher course in Yorkshire, and the storm never reached further than London. Many thousands, if not millions of trees had been brought down throughout the South-East of England and London.

Drama accompanied the storm. Lissie was still attending Kent College in Pembury at the time, and she used to come home by train with either Margaret or me picking her up at the station in Staplehurst, about ten miles south of our house. I only heard about the drama that ensued the next day by phone.

On this night of the storm, when it had already begun raining buckets, Lissie 'chose' not to get off the train at her usual Staplehurst Station. Margaret telephoned the school and they said she had certainly left. This left Margaret in a state of panic, which was natural. In addition, she had arranged to pick up Madeleine from her school in Maidstone.

Eventually, Margaret received a phone call saying that Lissie had alighted at the next station, with her friend. They had been chatting and overlooked their station, so got out at the next one. A car driver had seen two children walking in the pouring rain, but he was nervous as to whether he should stop for them, presumably fearing they would panic. He had then stopped at the next house to alert the owner that two children would be passing by. The house was the family home of the friend Lissie was with, and the owner then phoned Margaret who arranged to pick up Lissie. All was sorted out, but not before a few very terrifying hours for Margaret, which added to my guilt at not being there.

An amusing incident occurred involving Madeleine, not that she recalls it with anything other than acute embarrassment. When she was around the age of 14/15, she had gone down to town with some friends and spent the evening in a local pub. At some point in the evening, we had a phone call asking us to collect her. When we arrived, we saw her sitting on the pavement outside the pub, sobbing, 'I am so sorry, Daddy' again and again. She was very, very pissed!

Another lovely memory for me is the evening we first agreed that Lissie could go to town by herself. We did not suggest a time when we expected her back, leaving it to her to decide. The bus would normally take about nine or ten minutes to get to the centre of town. At around 10.45, she phoned to ask if and when she should be back. Using every bit of my many years of accumulated psychological wisdom, I replied that it was entirely up to her. She arrived home within 10 -15 minutes! Brilliant psychology!

Another incident also involved Lissie. I was walking down Gabriel's Hill in the centre of Maidstone and happened to glance through the window of a small café as I was passing. I saw Lissie sitting at a table with three scruffy looking boys. She saw me at the same time as I saw her. In the instance I saw her, I also noticed a vanishing left hand, which moved out of sight in what seemed like less than a nanosecond. (A nanosecond is a unit of time equal to a billionth of a second.) But, quick as it moved, it did not move quickly enough. I had seen it! A cigarette in her left hand! I howled with laughter (quietly to myself) while I continued down Gabriel's Hill, but I don't think Lissie was quite as amused.

Keeping up the garden and mowing the lawn was hard work but worthwhile. Particularly so when Madeleine decided to get married. The local parish church was a perfect medieval church for the wedding itself, but we decided – provided the weather held up – our garden would provide the perfect venue for the wedding reception.

On the day itself, the weather was perfect except for some local thunderstorms, but these stayed away from our garden. We managed, or rather Margaret managed, to provide most of the food, plus we ordered in some, including two lovely huge pork pies. As soon as they were brought out, all the elderly male relatives (Chris's relatives, I should add) ate the lot in about two seconds. But thankfully, the whole event went well. We had hired a classical music group and a jazz band that played throughout, and I gave my 'father of the bride speech'. I was very nervous, but I got through it.

I commented in my speech that Chris had given in his notice to the Royal Navy, and for his punishment had been sent to the Falklands for six months. But some time after he got back, he had replies from all the three or four universities he had applied to, all offering him a place. He chose Cardiff. Madeleine had obtained her first post as a lawyer in a Cardiff firm of solicitors, and after Chris graduated, they bought a house there.

Lissie and Marcus had met by this time and also bought their first house in Cardiff. With both Lissie and Madeleine and their partners living in Cardiff, Margaret and myself had a big decision to make. The journey from Maidstone to the Welsh capital was long and tiring, even though it was all by motorway. Since we both liked to visit them, we pondered over whether it would be sensible to sell our house in Maidstone and move to the west. After her first post in Cardiff, Madeleine obtained a job within a Bristol-based firm of solicitors, and Chris found a teaching post also in the Bristol area. So, with Lissie and Marcus staying in Cardiff, this led us to sell our house in Maidstone and making a move down to the West Country.

Maidstone itself was the County Town of Kent, and had its share of beautiful medieval buildings such as the parish church,

Bishop's Palace and stables, but with typically narrow-minded local authority members. Culturally, there was little there. At some point in the past, Maidstone had 'developed' the road system by creating a new road that ran between the medieval church and the Bishop's Palace on the one side and its beautiful medieval stables on the other, destroying the unity of the whole area.

Another example of the small minds on the council was even more pathetic. Maidstone Council was discussing the building of a large leisure complex, to include a swimming pool and gym. But they also discussed whether they should incorporate a state-of-the-art concert hall. The Lady Mayor at the time was reported in the local newspaper to have commented that she was only interested in large show bands, such as the German 'George Last Big Band', and why on earth did you need a state-of-the-art concert hall for that! In the end, they built a pathetic small hall with a few raised seats! The rest of the leisure complex and swimming pool was fine, but it meant that the county town of Kent – just like all the other towns in the very large county of Kent – does not have a quality concert hall to this day. But this is the plight of all towns within a 40-50-mile radius of London.

While I liked Kent, particularly its proximity to France, I put up with Maidstone. Margaret was less keen, though, and was pleased to move away when we did. We did, however, both miss the easy short trips to France. All the wine and champagne we provided for Madeleine and Chris's wedding was bought from a retailer in Montreuil, near Boulogne.

In 2001, we bought a house in Portishead, near Bristol, and situated on the Bristol Channel, but did not move in until the following year. In the summer of 2001, in what was to be our last summer in Maidstone, Margaret and I, Madeleine and Chris, Lissie and Marcus, all went to Vent, in the Oeztal region of Tyrol, to do some climbing. We had hired a mountain guide, and I hoped to re-create the wonderful climbing holiday I'd spent with my mother and Toni in the summer of 1958, but hopefully without the 'near death' experience of that occasion which I described earlier.

Margaret did not climb with us, as she had suffered a minor heart condition the previous year. I am sure she could have managed, but she felt not. Madeleine had also damaged her knee in a fall just before we left England, and although she tried to go with us on the first training day, she found it too uncomfortable. This was a great disappointment for her and for the rest of us. So that left Lissie, Marcus, Chris, and me.

We started out on the first day on what was to prove a very, very long hike up to the first mountain hut. Margaret and Madeleine accompanied us for around an hour and then turned back, while the rest of us carried on with our guide. Eventually, we arrived at one of the highest mountain huts in that part of the Alps. We sat down to eat, but after about one mouthful, I could not manage any more, I was just too exhausted. That night, it was alleged that I snored so loudly that some Dutch girls, who were on their first mountain climb, could not sleep. Eventually one of them cried, 'I want to go home.' The chap below me was doing most of the snoring.

The following day was an extremely long one, climbing up one mountain and then passing the area where many years before an arm of a very dead body had appeared, sticking out of the receding ice field. This was the 'Oetzi' man, who was found to have been lying there for around 5/6000 years and had only been discovered due to the melting ice.

When we got to the site, there was no snow or ice to be seen anywhere, but we saw the memorial that had been erected. We went on an ever-lengthening walk to our next destination. On the way, I identified the Fineispitz, the very same mountain that had terrified me in 1958 with its covering of ice all the precipitous way up to the very top. Now, though, there was no snow or ice to be seen. Global warming deniers, please note.

This reminds me that throughout those few days, I had repeatedly said to our guide that I hoped he would not take us up the steep ice slope on the way to the summit of the Wildspitz. He always reacted as if he had no idea what I was talking about. So, on the last day, having slept at the same mountain hut where I had stayed with my mother and Toni all those years ago (in the room next to the poor young man who died of pulmonary embolism), we set out to climb the Wildspitz.

We duly started out on our climb to the top, and I recognised the route the guide was taking us. To my horror, it was the very same route that would take us to the ice wall. But when we got to this fearsome ice wall, there was not a trace of ice! I relaxed. Again, global warming deniers, please note. However, I shouldn't have relaxed.

We went on up and eventually arrived at the last almost perpendicular rock face to the summit. I am not sure just how long this last stretch was, but it could have been around 100 to 200 feet at the very least, and possibly quite a bit more. What was scary was that it was not a solid continuous large mass of solid rock, but over the years it had been broken up by continuous expansion and contraction into large individual slabs of rock. Most were solidly embedded and/or iced together, which made climbing fairly easy, but many of these rock slabs were quite loose and would shift as we put our weight on them. Scary. It also suggests that over the next century or so, these rocks will slowly fall off, so eventually the mountain peak will be considerably lower – and then the Wildspitz might no longer be the second highest mountain in Austria!

What happened next was to prove the most terrifying part of the whole four days, and much worse than my 1968 ice-field climb. We came down from the peak onto a glacier, until the guide stopped for what I assumed was a break. It happened to be on the edge of a vertical cliff that disappeared into oblivion, or at least from view after about 20 feet. It was so steep. Ahead of us, I saw to my consternation that a group of climbers (who had, in fact, been at the very first mountain hut we'd slept in) had been roped up together and then disappeared one by one down over the edge – into oblivion. How could they do it? Never in a million years could or would I ever manage to commit suicide in just such a way.

When we had finished our drinks, the guide uncoiled his rope and proceeded to attach each of us to it. No, no, no! We were to follow down this vertical precipice! I am sure Chris, Marcus, and Lissie were horrified as well, but nobody dared admit it. They all pretended it was fine (ha-ha! If you believe that you will... Oh, well.). Chris was sent over the top first, then me, Lissie, and then Marcus, with the guide holding up the end of the rope. I noticed that the guide was always very careful to attach his rope to some solid rock as we slowly descended, one at a time. But, at one point, in order to get from one of his footholds to the next, our guide unhitched the rope from the retaining rock, and with no further rope support, jumped down to the next projecting foothold. Just another 'what if'.

Eventually, we got down, to my relief at least. The others pretended to take the whole thing in their stride; just another day at the office. Again, you can believe that if you like! We then all walked along to the mountain hut we had left that morning, emptied the cellars, and continued down to be greeted by Margaret and Madeleine, then drank a well-earned pint or two, or perhaps three, of Gluhwein.

It was nevertheless a fantastic trip... after it was over. I felt so sorry for Madeleine, as I am sure she would have managed it comfortably if it had not been for her prior injury. However, would she have been even more terrified than I was, climbing down, or rather being winched and lowered down that precipice (or as it seemed, under-hanging precipice) of one mile (at least)? Well, perhaps not a complete mile! After the ordeal was over, everyone (except me) continued to pretend it was all a piece of cake. What liars.

Madeleine and Christopher: wedding day.. 2000

CHAPTER 12

Portishead and North Somerset

We returned home: Madeleine and Chris, Lissie and Marcus to Cardiff, and Margaret and me to Maidstone. Both Madeleine and Chris had found jobs – Madeleine in Bristol practising law, and Chris teaching in North Somerset – so we came down to Portishead to help them in their house-hunting.

While there, we noticed some homes being built, or Lissie had seen a house in the process of being built. Or another version is that the saleslady in a building site office suggested we look at some houses being built, as part of a terrace. Whatever the correct version of history, we viewed the buildings and were shown one completed show house, then viewed another house still not completed internally. We decided there and then to buy, and we have never regretted this decision. We had originally decided to buy and then to 'let' the house, as we were not quite ready to leave Loose, but in the end we changed our minds, sold our Loose house, and moved down. It meant we were near to Madeline and Chris, who were also in Portishead, and Lissie and Marcus in Cardiff. No more long motorway journeys.

The process of selling our Loose house had its odd moments. I had taken the precaution of covering up a few dodgy gaps in the cellar with fill-in cement. One middle-aged couple liked the house and arranged for a structural survey, but the result alarmed then somewhat. No doubt they expected a 200-year-old house to be in perfect order and just like new. They backed off, but then asked the estate agents to pass on a request for us to pay half their survey fees. Joke. We saw their surveyor later, who had incidentally also surveyed the house when we moved in, and told him of this strange request to halve costs of the survey. His comment was what on earth should anyone expect of a house every bit of 200 years old.

We moved into our new house in Portishead in March 2002. In May 2002, Annabelle was born – the first of four grandchildren. Margaret and I became grandparents, yet it seemed only yesterday when we two had met.

We were able to help out with babysitting while Madeleine went back to work, and later this included picking up Annabelle from her nursery. I will never forget the very first afternoon when we came to collect her. Madeleine had taken her there, but Margaret and I collected her at the end of the day. We saw her sitting on a cushion together with a staff member, but as soon as she saw us, she burst into teas and rushed into my arms! She must have been there all day, fearing she had been abandoned. We then had the delightful duty of looking after William. So, we were kept busy with babysitting and loved every minute of it, as they were such lovely babies! Oh, how things change!

The year after we came to Portishead, we went for our first cruise holiday, from UK to Boston, but returning by air. We stayed for a while with my cousin Flora and her family, then we drove up into the depths of Maine to stay with Flora's parents, Silvio and Trudy, in their summer home situated by a lake. The visit was lovely.

To reminisce – throughout my life, my mother had always taken care to sweep up any crumbs on the dining table while we were all still eating, or just at the end, but with her hands, not with a brush. I had caught the habit, to the annoyance of just about everyone, especially Margaret, Madeleine, and Elisabeth. When we were dining with Silvio and Trudy, what should Silvio do at the end of the meal but sweep up the crumbs! Margaret and I both started laughing. It was always clear to me that this must have been a long-established family habit, going back at least to my grandparents, but who knows how far further it went back? Silvio was not sure. I suspect Trudy was just as irritated by Silvio's habit, but constrained herself in front of her guests! Unfortunately, neither Madeleine nor Lissie have caught the habit, to the detriment of their dining tables.

The above was our first cruise, courtesy of the Royal Caribbean International Line, and which we enjoyed. Later, we booked a three-week cruise to Greenland on the Discovery Liner – sadly, no longer in existence – with one-day stops at the Faroe Islands and Iceland, and then Cork, Ireland, on the way back. On one of our port visits in Greenland, we saw a Post Office where 'Father Christmas' was in attendance, or so it was said. In spite of not actually seeing him (he must have been visiting somewhere), he did manage to sign and send a postcard each to Annabelle and William. I am afraid both Sam and Rosa missed out on this treat, as they were not yet born.

What was noticeable about Greenland was the enormous and obvious disparity between the standard of living and standard of housing between the resident native population and the Danish immigrants and officials who ran the place. So, nothing new there then. But it did leave a rather sour note with us.

Also very evident was another example of climate change. At one of the three towns on the West Coast where the cruise ship stopped, we were able to go on a boat trip to the head of the local fjord. I recall the boat's captain telling us that the fjord had been navigable for its entire length of 50 miles, up to the end of the glacier. But at the time of our visit, ice from the glacier had filled up the entire length of the fjord and then emerged as huge icebergs. Again, global warming deniers, take note. But in compensation for not being able to cruise up the fjord, the guide stopped the boat, scooped up some floating ice, melted it, and mixed it with some gin and gave us each a small drink, saying we were now drinking melted ice that had fallen as snow some 30 million years before. Wow! We cruised past giant icebergs which, close up, were simply stunning in the glinting sun.

Our next cruise was on the *Cunard Queen Mary 2* to New York, where we stayed for a few days and flew back, to be followed by a return cruise from Southampton to New York, staying in New York for a few days, and also on the Cunard Queen Mary 2. Let me impart some advice to new would-be cruisers. When each party books, they are asked what eating arrangements they would like. The various options are for each couple to eat on their own for each meal, or to choose to eat at a table for four, or six, or eight. The company then attempts to match up the guests so that they all have something in common. This works quite well, but on our Iceland tour, we opted for a table of four. The other couple were a retired medical consultant and his wife, a social worker. Meals were very pleasant, but towards the end of three weeks we really ended up with little to talk about, having said it all. I recommend a table of eight.

Lissie and Marcus married in March 2005. However, we no longer had our large Loose garden, so we could not repeat the kind of reception which Madeleine and Chris had. They booked the then very new St David's Hotel in Cardiff Bay and it was a lovely wedding, but I am afraid that for whatever reason I could not put together a speech I was happy with. I struggled with it, but nothing really worked. My apologies to Lissie and Marcus.

I never knew what anyone thought of my effort at speechifying at Madeleine and Chris's wedding, but years later, Marcus said it had not only been extremely good, but the best he had ever heard! Flattering, and it cheered me up, but he then added that my speech for his wedding was not nearly as good! He was quite correct, and this comment made me feel as bad as I had originally, but it was fair and accurate. Apologies once again! If I had the time again, I am sure I could have done so much better. However, it was a lovely day, and I hope everyone left happy. Judging by the amount of alcohol consumed, I think it is safe to say they did.

Eventually, of course, Sam arrived on the scene. I vividly recall the day he was born, as Margaret and I were waiting outside the maternity and delivery wards in the corridor for what seemed like hours. It *was* hours. We eventually saw Marcus walk out of the delivery ward with Sam cradled in his arms, and it was then another good hour, if not more, before we were allowed to see Lissie, Marcus, and Sam. All was well, of course, except for Margaret and I. Our birth experience had been traumatic. Next was the birth of Rosa, which went much more smoothly, and we were not kept nearly as long to see mother and child – and Marcus!

In the years since, Sam and Rosa have been as delightful as Annabelle and William had been. (And still are!) Given the distance from Portishead to Cardiff, we were not able to babysit as we had for Annabelle and William, but initially Margaret stayed for two nights a week to look after Rosa and collect Sam from school. It was while staying in Cardiff to look after Rosa that she suffered some attack that could have been a heart attack, but was later diagnosed differently. She was taken to hospital, where she stayed for a few days. This was traumatic for Lissie and the children, but she was in good hands and has not suffered any reoccurrence.

Later, I stayed overnight with them on some occasions. One of my memories in particular is picking up Rosa from her first infant school and experiencing her delight in seeing us. She would always run over and jump into my arms. She hasn't done it since! To compensate for not living close, we continued to go to Cardiff to pick up Sam and Rosa from their school one day each week.

After one night sleeping with them, Rosa came up and crept into my bed and cuddled up. She then asked if I would stay overnight the following week. We did, and she came up and crept into my bed. But never again! Had I been sweating a bit too much and had the very slightest of aromas, so she was put off?

Three particular memories involving birthday celebrations stand out after we moved to Portishead. The first was for my 70th birthday. Margaret, Christine, and I were walking to the 'Olive Tree' restaurant alongside Bristol Docks, and I was becoming increasingly irritated at how very slowly they were walking, as we were already late. I knew we were going for lunch but not why. When we arrived, both Annabelle and William, who were sitting with an empty chair between them, jumped up and down, screaming with delight when I appeared. (They have never done it since.) The next particular memory is our celebration of Margaret's 60th birthday celebrations at Raymond Blanc's two Michelin-starred restaurant, *Le Manoir aux Quat'Saisons*, in Oxfordshire. What an amazing experience. Perhaps it should be repeated sometime? The other is an equally memorable experience at the Restaurant Hywel Jones, by Lucknam Park, for my 75th birthday. The way they looked after us in our own exclusive dining room was just lovely.

A consequence of moving away from Kent was that I had to give up the sessions I provided to GPs in Snodland and Walderslade, and from the sessions I provided in the two private Hospitals. But I then managed to negotiate sessions in the (private) BUPA Hospital in Bristol, which involved a weekly afternoon and occasional evening sessions. I also kept on my appointments at Harley Street. Referrals mostly came from the same source as before, namely solicitors and solicitors agents who were seeking reports in connection with personal injury. There was also an increase in referrals in connection with Family Law issues.

On one memorable occasion, I had a direct telephone call from a Family Court Judge. While still in Maidstone, I had seen five siblings who were claiming mistreatment. The court case was held, and I thought nothing more of it. But then I had a call from the Judge who had presided over the case the first time, asking if I would be prepared to revisit and re-assess all the children and the family situation. This was the only time a Judge had acted in such a way, and it was interesting, as normally expert witnesses do not get that much feedback from the Judge. I assumed he had been impressed with my earlier report.

Along with many hundreds of personal injury cases, I saw a series of 59 men referred from one firm of solicitors over a ten-year period, in connection with claims for injury suffered by men while teenagers residing in care homes. I also saw just one woman with similar claims. The men had all been removed from their homes because of parental neglect or abuse, leading them to become out of control. They had been placed into care homes for their protection and in the hope that good and loving care would lead to improvement in their behaviour.

All these individuals then complained about further abuse within the various care homes they were placed into, most complaining of sexual abuse. Apart from five cases, all claims against the respective care homes were accepted and compensation paid. But after a change in the management of one local authority that had been responsible for running two of the care homes complained of, the authority decided to fight the claims, so I then found myself up against the local authority-appointed medical witness. He argued that as these men had been out of control as young lads when living at home, they must have been 'psychopathic', rather than normal lads who became out of control following abuse or neglect at their family home. Therefore, he argued that if their behaviour in care homes had become worse, it must have been the result of the same psychopathic tendencies within themselves. This was a typical medical diagnosis of 'illness', wherein the problem resides firmly 'within' the individual's genes or some such mechanisms, as opposed to a psychological interplay between the individual and his/her home or environment.

Another way of describing the problem is to say that the psychiatric view describes the 'observable' behavioural characteristics of an individual and then devises endless diagnostic categories of psychopathy based on such observable behaviour, but which in fact says nothing whatsoever about 'why' such observable behaviour has developed – other than the assumption it must be to do with genes or some such mechanism.

I am glad to say he modified his views somewhat after he had read my reports! I taught him the difference between 'illness', or 'observable behaviour', and a psychological argument of 'why' such problem behaviour had developed, with the argument that if the family home or environment had been abusive or causing problems sufficient to place the lad in a care home, then further mistreatment and/or abuse could, and in all probability would, cause further psychological harm while in that care home. Further neglect/abuse/poor care would only make the boys' behaviour worse. It was a pleasing victory for me, but two of these men lost their claims in court. Judges still have a tendency to defer to medical opinion and appear to take little account of underlying family/environmental-type issues. Instead, 'a thief is a thief', and little else matters.

Other referrals came from GPs or self-referrals. I should recount one such self-referral, as it spoke so eloquently of a dire situation with some Child Clinical Psychologists, or more probably the established medical consensus within Child and Adolescent Mental Health Services. A mother referred herself to me in connection with her 8/9-year-old son. As she was paying herself, thus not being covered by insurance, I asked if she had been to her GP for a referral within the NHS. She said she had, and had been referred to the local Child & Adolescent Mental Health Service. She said she arrived on the appointed day, made herself known to the receptionist, and was asked to wait in the waiting room. After a while, a woman came to collect her son and took him into a room down the corridor. After 45 minutes, this same woman brought him back and arranged another appointment. She said this conversation about a new appointment was the only communication she had from the woman, who she presumed was the therapist. So she was left not knowing what they thought the problem was; if it was treatable; what, if anything, she might have got wrong at home; or how the child was like at home; or what she should or could be doing at home after treatment. So she left and never went back. This was, and still is, an all-too-common problem in children's units. Awful. Treating the child as if they were 'the problem' or 'ill". Why can't psychologists learn the difference between a psychological view of causation and medical models of illness? It's just ignorance of all psychological research has learned about child development over the last 100 years.

This problem, and apparent ignorance of child development, leads me to comment upon the history of Clinical Psychology as applied to the NHS and to education by Educational Psychologists. This is the failure to prepare psychologists with an understanding of and sufficient experience in examining children in the contexts of their upbringing and their families, which I contend has resulted in an over-reliance on psychometric testing – the skills that led to the development of the profession in the 1940s, 1950s, and 1960s.

The consequence has been that the interaction between the child and parent(s) is ignored, both within the NHS and in many Children's Units, and when such psychologists are instructed by the courts to prepare a psychological assessment of a parent's parenting ability or of a child's safety, they have no recourse other than to administer psychometric tests. No psychometric test currently in existence measures the relevant issues required by the court, which is: Is the parenting good enough? One could well ask why then would such unqualified psychologists agree to take instructions from the family courts. The answer, I suggest, is 'money'. In a case that went to the Appeal Court, an individual not central to the case had to submit to nine hours of (totally unnecessary) psychometric testing. At a few hundred pounds an hour, one can see the attraction!

The above reminds me of a weekend refresher course I attended in 2001, while I was still living in Maidstone. I saw an advert for a weekend course to be held at Oxford on the subject of behavioural therapy developments in the treatment of children. I had not known that there were any such developments, so I enrolled. The first talk was given by a university-based psychologist in charge of the children's section at one of our universities' Clinical Psychology courses. She began her talk, and I confess I immediately concluded that there were no new developments in the treatment of children. I knew all of her examples in the 1960s.

After about 20 minutes, a young woman sitting in front of me put her hand up and asked, 'Do you ever see the mothers?' Within what seemed like one-hundredth of a second, the lecturer barked, 'No, of course not. That would be to blame the parent!' I was shocked, and I am sure the questioner was, too. Nobody – the questioner, me, nor anyone else – could collect their thoughts and challenge this bit of ignorant nonsense. If questioning the parent is to blame them, then not questioning them is avoiding blaming them. But questioning them or not, they are still the same parent. In all the hundreds of hours I have seen and questioned a parent, I have never blamed a single one.

One questions a parent in order to get a history and account of their child, who they themselves have brought to the GP, asking for help. On many occasions, questioning the parent leads to advice which often solves the problem. In other cases, questioning the parent leads to delving into the parent's own childhood experiences, helping them confront very difficult experiences they had as a child. Successfully dealing with these often sorts out problems they are having with their own child. Blame is never involved. I am aware I am beginning to preach, but it is this poor training in some aspects of psychology that has led to poor work by some, and I stress, only *some* psychologists. Postgraduate training courses need to be aware.

I should mention some further work I did over the years for the British Psychological Society after I retired from the NHS. Up until 2009, the Society functioned as the regulatory body for its members. This function had been fiercely resisted for years, up until the late 1960s, by the Society's university membership. They clearly felt themselves above regulation. Eventually however, the membership agreed to the Society carrying out this function, which was, and had always been, essential for the protection of the public.

This meant that members of the public could complain to the Society about any psychologist, provided the psychologist was a member of the Society. When complaints from the public came in, the secretariat weeded out any trivial complaints, but for others the procedure was for the Society to set up a panel of three senior members to examine the complaint in the first instance. I had been involved in this task since 1990, and in ever increasing numbers after I retired. It had its onerous side but was an eye-opener into what a few supposedly adult and intelligent individual psychologists could get up to. However, most of the actual complaints were felt to be irrelevant and about issues which the society was not concerned with, such as complaints that were really about the complainant having lost a case in court and blaming the psychologist involved. The real problem was poor psychological work that the public were simply not aware of and so would not complain. This regulatory function was then taken over by a new NHS organisation after 2009/10.

In 2006, The British Psychological Society appointed me to represent the Society on the Royal Courts of Justice 'Family Justice Council Expert Witness Sub-Committee'. This involved about four trips a year to the High Court in The Strand. Representatives of all the main medical specialities that provided regular reports for the Family Courts were involved. This was fascinating work, but also interesting in that we got to see the Judges' chambers and meeting rooms that one would otherwise never see. Lord-Justice Thorpe chaired these meetings. A second psychologist was also appointed to represent the Society on this committee, namely Jane Ireland, Professor of Forensic Psychology in the University of Central Lancashire. In 2006, I had also been asked by the Society to sit on its own BPS Professional Practice Board Expert Witness Advisory Group. This body advised the Society and its members on all appropriate psychological practice and Involvement in court work.

In the few years Prof. Ireland and I had been members of this RCJ Committee, various reports and queries had been sent to this committee for advice and comment. Some involved psychologists, and all of these showed up some very questionable and poor work. My involvement with the British Psychological Society's regulatory function had, as mentioned above, also alerted me to some very poor work, and in one case very questionable personal conduct. In the course of her work, Jane Ireland had also had experience of similar poor work sent to her for comment.

I had previously had court experience of some really inadequate work by a psychologist acting on behalf of a young woman/new mother. His report terrified the woman as a result of a wholly unjustified use of a psychometric test that was still in the process of being constructed. It was a test that would hopefully be able to determine the possibility of rehabilitation of hard-core long-term prisoners. No-one in this case was a long-term prisoner. The case simply concerned a mother, her new-born baby, and her unwillingness to allow the father to visit their child. Its wholly invalid conclusions that the father was a psychopath, based on a test that was entirely inappropriate, terrified the mother.

So, both Jane Ireland and I were aware of very poor psychological work being presented to the courts, often in the use of entirely inappropriate psychometric tests, particularly intelligence tests. And we were certainly not alone in this judgment. In an Appeal Court Judgment, one of the Appeal Court Judges commented on the wholly unjustified use of nine hours of psychometric tests, including an intelligence test administered to an individual not central to the case. In addition, the Appeal Court Judge made the following comment: 'Family Courts do not remove children from their parents into care because the parents in question are not intelligent enough to care for them or have low intelligence quotas. Children are only removed into care: (1) if they are suffering or likely to suffer significant harm in the care of their parents; and (2) if it is in their interests that a care order is made. Anything else is social engineering and wholly impermissible.'

At one meeting, we were informed that the Family Division of the High Court had some funds available to finance any appropriate research involving the Family Court system, and we were all asked if we wanted to submit a research project.

I jumped at the chance. After discussion with Jane Ireland, I said I would present a brief outline of a research project. This was accepted, and so Jane Ireland agreed to write it up as a formal, fully worked-out research project, which was presented to the Family Division of the High Court, and it was agreed. The project involved the proposal that four experienced psychologists should examine psychological reports that had been presented to a Family Court in connection with family parenting issues. We proposed going to courts to examine historical records. The Secretariat then arranged for this to happen, and three courts agreed to let us in. Jane Ireland and I, plus two other psychologists, then went to these courts and spent a whole day in each one, looking at the case files that had involved psychological reports.

Both Prof. Ireland and I anticipated that we would see a few poor reports that would be below standard, but we were shocked at the actual findings, which showed approximately 50% of the 100 reports we examined were on a sliding scale from fairly poor to awful. A large proportion of these reports judged to be poor had administered psychometric tests, and almost all of these included an intelligence test. They were clearly not aware of the Court of Appeal Judgement I quoted above.

The report was published and was warmly received by the legal establishment, with Jane Ireland, the named author, being rightly congratulated by many judges and psychologists. However, the report also resulted in hysteria from a very few psychologists who, one can only presume, feared for their careers as expert witnesses. Three psychologists then put in a formal complaint against Jane Ireland to the regulatory body, citing eight serious individual complaints, all of which were summarily dismissed when the case came to a formal hearing. My opinion was that these complainants disgraced themselves.

So, just what was the real issue that caused so much of what I can only call 'hysteria' that led to their complaints? I believe that the complainants were all heavy users of psychometric tests. My interpretation and conclusions of the various reports that I read in the above study is that those reports which impressed me seemed to indicate that the psychologist writing the report had had extensive experience of seeing children and their parents, and whose reports were informed by this experience of theirs, so they were able to give appropriate comments and, if asked, advice to the courts without the administration of any unnecessary psychometric tests. So, why was the outcry so vehement?

My conclusion was simple, even though critics would no doubt call it cynical. Those psychologists who had little experience of seeing children and their families for psychological treatment had little to go on if they wished to take court referrals. Of huge significance is that all such work is carried out privately, often by psychologists who have had NHS experience and then left/retired and continued to work, but privately, or some who have always worked privately from qualification. Either way, private income was the main, or significant source of income, and thus essential for the psychologist concerned.

It could take up to three hours to administer, score, report on, and type up the result of just one test. Adding up the hours it would take to administer, score, and report on two, or three, or four or more tests, adds up to quite a few hours. As mentioned, all court work is done privately and thus charged for. Add up the total hours at maybe £500 an hour or more, and it can be understood that this work could be called a 'nice little earner'! The more tests administered, the 'nicer' the earner. Cynical? Possibly. But cynics can sometimes be right.

Another interesting issue that I have never heard commented upon, other than in its immediate aftermath, and which may have some relevance to the above, is the publication and reforms outlined in the 'Wolf Report' around 1995/6, The above issues of arguably poor psychologist reports may well have been a long-term result of this report.

Lord Justice Wolf presented a report that included comments and recommendations concerning perceived or unconscious bias in some experts' reports, leading to these experts being called 'The Hired Gun'. The situation prior to this report was such that solicitors representing one side of a disputed case requested a medical/expert report, and the opposing side may or may not have instructed their own medical expert. The perception was that these 'medical expert reports' would tend to favour the side from whom they were instructed, i.e. 'The Hired Gun'. The Wolf Report proposed that this should end, and instead a single expert only should be instructed and only 'by the Court', and therefore the report had to be provided 'to the Court', and not to one side of a dispute/issue or the other, thus not favouring one side or another. These criticisms of the 'hired gun' applied predominantly to the medical specialists who were involved in giving evidence to the Civil, Criminal, and Family Courts much more frequently than psychologists.

I have seen no public comments on this Wolf Report decision, other than in the immediate aftermath of its publication, when I recall there was general agreement. No doubt, the 'hired gun' is a practice of the past. But I am left wondering if the poor psychological practices I have mentioned above have flourished because there is only the single 'expert' in any court case, with no (potentially) contrary and informed and knowledgeable opposition, which would surely concentrate the minds of each 'expert'. There may be no bias, or 'hired gun' any more, as there undoubtedly had been, but no professionally informed challenges from another psychologist either.

My comments above on the earning potentials of psychologists when administering psychological tests in court work may reflect on another example of the corruption of money. There was a big fuss after 'Failing Grayling' – otherwise known as Christopher Grayling, Conservative Member of Parliament, and Conservative Lord Chancellor in David Cameron's Government – cut back the amount of finance available for Legal Aid, a device so incredibly important to individuals or families brought before the court. Psychologists wished to protest. It was entirely appropriate for psychologists to protest at the diminishing amounts of finance that was to be made available to assist families in their defence. Few, if any, families had sufficient funds to enable them to fund their own defence, and when the issue was the continued parenting of their children, nothing could be more important than that these families obtain expert legal and professional support.

A group of around 50 psychologists duly prepared a solution they hoped would be approved by the British Psychological Society, who would then publish the letter and send it to the Lord Chancellor's Department and to the Government. The proposed letter said quite properly that this proposal would greatly diminish financial assistance for families when taken to court. They proposed a solution: 'experienced' psychologists who were instructed to prepare a Court Report would vet the case and if, in their opinion, it was a trivial family case, they would approach an 'inexperienced' psychologist to examine the family and then put in a much cheaper invoice. They then suggested that this allowed 'serious problems' to be seen by experienced psychologists, who would of course present their usual much higher fees. Hilarious! Grotesque!

I replied. I gently, or not so gently, pointed out that the concept of a 'trivial' family case that came before the courts was a self-contradiction. No case that came before the Family Court involving a family, with the possibility of the parents losing control or care of their children until the age of 16 or having them permanently adopted, was 'trivial'. Furthermore, how could any psychologist know just what was involved in a family case until the psychologist was appointed by the court, and then sent ALL the papers, as distinct from a brief outline asking of their availability from a solicitor. So, how could judgements be made as to whether an experienced, i.e. 'high earning' psychologist, should be involved, or just an inexperienced 'low worth' (sorry, low earning) psychologist be given the brief. They made a serious mistake. They circulated their proposal by e-mail, and I was included in the circulation. I replied ridiculing the proposal, sending my reply to the same list.

All letters that purported to represent the British Psychological Society had to be seen and approved by the President of the Society. I could not be confident that this lunatic group would instead send out such a proposal directly to the Lord Chancellor's office without gaining approval, and so drawing ridicule upon the Society. So I took it upon myself to alert the President of the BPS, sending her a copy of these proposals. The nonsense letter was never sent! The group of 50 or so were outraged. Tough. I did my duty. I was erased from their e-mail list.

After a long shift, I finally gave up all psychological work on 30 September, 2013, exactly 50 years after I started clinical training in Manchester on 1st October, 1963. I had thoroughly enjoyed every minute of those 50 years of work, even though some aspects over the years had proved to be difficult, and some decisions particularly difficult in their consequences for Margaret. For her continued support, I am so immensely grateful.

Throughout those 50 years, I have always felt huge gratitude to, and owe an enormous 'Thank You' to Reading University and Prof. Magdalene Vernon for accepting me on her psychology course in 1960. That single decision transformed my life.

Retirement has its compensations, but approaching memory failure is not one of them – even if, at this stage, it is not too noticeable. I doubt if I would be able to undertake any psychological therapy now, although I suspect this is more due to having had enough and losing the motivation than it is to memory failure, but I do miss the contact with other psychologists. I have been on the e-mail address list of the Clinical Psychology Department at Bath University, which keeps me in touch with developments, and hopefully helps to keep any memory loss at bay.

One such contact was to volunteer to participate in the initial short-listing of applicants to the University Clinical Psychology Course. When I last became involved in shortlisting in the 1970s, this was a fairly non-stressful activity, as we would be lucky if there were more than 8-10 applicants, if that. Bath University was facing the problem of over 400 applicants for 17 places, so engaging the help of many external psychologists made sense. It kept me in touch, but it was hard work keeping to the complicated format the university had developed. What was so dispiriting was to see that unless an applicant had had something approaching a minimum of 4-5 years of experience of working as a psychology assistant, or as an NHS or similar employee following their university undergraduate course, they had no chance of getting acceptance on the course. Many candidates had many more years of paid work as psychology assistants. Many had an MA, degree and some even a Ph.D. I was one of two candidates when I was accepted in 1963! And immediately from university! That would be impossible now. Have I been any worse as a psychologist as any of the lucky new graduates will turn out to be? Maybe in 50 years' time there will be an answer.

While on the subject of Bath University, I decided to attend the end-of-course presentations given by the newly graduating Clinical Psychologists two years ago. They all presented their various research projects undertaken as part of their course. A few outlined projects with children, but never made any reference to the existence of parents, never mind actually seeing them, which was very dispiriting. However, one student did mention having carried out a treatment project with children, and referred to the fact that she had involved and seen their mothers. It was an impressive presentation in its own rights, but mentioning mothers was a bonus, and I applauded her work after she had finished, saying how unusual and how refreshing it was to see that she recognised that children did have mothers. I noticed that she blushed, but she was clearly pleased.

I obviously mentioned the above presentation and its reference to the existence of parents because it chimed with my work with children and their parents. But it reminded me then of the very basic philosophy of that department, which I believe is the most stringent of all the Clinical Psychology Post-Graduate courses in its reverence for and compliance with what is the NHS catch phrase – 'Evidence-based therapy'. Of course this is appropriate, but it raises so many questions.

In the field of children, all the academic evidence obtained in a century of research into child and personality development demonstrates the influence of the family, the environment, and even the culture. It seems to me that this leads to one obvious conclusion: to ignore the parent(s) when treating a child is to ignore a century of evidence. If anyone should doubt this, they should ask themselves how it is that children born to English parents living in England grow up as typical English adults, and how it is that children born to a French family living in France is likely to grow up as a typical French adult. To ignore parents and parenting is simply stupid. But, as I have written in an earlier chapter, parents are so often completely ignored when seeing children for psychological help.

If I have one major regret in all the 50 years of working as a clinical psychologist, it is first of all not to have completed, or even properly commenced, the Ph.D. that I had registered to undertake with Leeds University in 1968. It could have given me the incentive to pursue research later on in the area of child and family work, or even to publish theoretical articles on the importance and necessity of involving a parent(s) when seeing a child. When this is done, it is obvious – or at least was to me – just how influential parents are in the behaviour, development, and outcome, for better or worse, of their child, and how they must be involved in any treatment. In some cases, they just need advice. In some other cases, they need to reset their views of how best to raise their child. In some cases, they need therapy themselves before they are ready to accept advice.

The need to follow 'evidence-based treatment' – the flavour of the month – should not be defined solely by following stringent research and then its publication. It can be the results obtained by observing the impact of treatment after having seen the parent(s) of referred children, and again and again, seeing the transformation in parenting when they have confronted their own, often deep-seated problems, which can go back to their own early childhoods. On many occasions, just confronting their own often deep-seated problems can alone transform how they, the parents, deal with their own children, to the latter's benefit. Therapy that works, even when giving simple advice, is 'evidence-based treatment'. In hundreds of families that I have seen over the years, I can confidently point to the success of so doing. I repeat, when seeing parents as well as seeing their child for treatment, and noting the beneficial result of so doing, is 'evidence-based', even if the results have not been published. If I have anything to contribute to Clinical Psychology, that is the message I would want to convey.

I could add here that the above is relevant to my criticism of those psychologists mentioned who, in my opinion, so disgraced themselves and their profession in their criticism of the research undertaken into the psychological examination and reporting of Family Court work. Too often it was clear just how little experience the psychologist had of any family intervention.

Elisabeth and Marcus: wedding day: 2005

CHAPTER 13

Further family memories

Peter Bally Snr. the husband of my mother's sister Annamirl, arranged a family gathering of the Pirquet families and their children and grandchildren every ten years in January, starting in 1973, initially to celebrate Annamirl's 60th birthday. They were held in Ebensee, which housed the largest hotel near Rindbach, where our grandfather had lived since the war, and where he retired to after having looked after the Pirquet Family Tree and Fruit Nursery in Hirschstetten.

Peter Bally paid for all hotel expenses, which was a lovely idea, even though for us the journey was in danger of breaking the bank! We had bought a VW 411 car not long beforehand, and this car was a nightmare in the wind, but served its purpose. It was an estate car, which came in very handy on this trip. We felt we could not afford a hotel on the journey down to Austria, so we stopped in a motorway picnic area for the night, putting Madeleine in the back with me, and a heavily pregnant Margaret in the front. It was freezing. I slept in the back, as I had to continue driving the next morning, otherwise it would and should have been Margaret.

The event went off well and was a good opportunity to meet up with the elder Pirquet siblings and our cousins. At the end of the long weekend, we thought we would have a few more days to ourselves before we drove back home, so headed north to a town called Freistadt, but found the hotels too expensive so we went further on towards the Czechoslovakian border and stayed at an inn/ guesthouse. We saved ourselves a few shillings, but we were the only guests. It was freezing, and to add to the difficulties, Madeleine decided to start teething, but only at night – and only when I was trying to get to sleep. But with some wonderful techniques, I managed to soothe her so that we both got some sleep. Ah. Despite the cold, the whole area was lovely.

We went to all three 10-year gatherings in Ebensee, again always paid for by Peter Bally (senior). After they came to an end, with the death of Peter and then Annamirl, we held a meeting in Hinterbruhl, near Vienna, where Florette, Franzl, and Elizabeth lived. This was the first 'public outing' for Annabelle, who looked the typical young Austrian in her dirndl!

Whenever we have been to Ebensee and Rindbach, we would invariably undertake a pilgrimage to the Gmunden Keramic factory and sales outlet in, surprisingly, Gmunden! The town is at the opposite end of the Traunsee, the other end being Ebensee and Rindbach. As well as invariably buying china for ourselves and Madeleine and Lissie, we would also go to the Konditorei, Schnellingers. It is situated near the centre of the town, on the lakefront. This is one of the well-known coffee and cake shops in Austria, and figures in my mother's memoirs, where she recounts being taken there by her father on special trips in the early 1900s. That it still exists is amazing. She also refers to special trips to the northeast side of the lake to a café where they make special cones of ice cream and whipped cream. She took us to this café on one of our trips to Rindbach. I remember the shape of this speciality but not the taste.

Reflecting on the previous pages, what jumps out is how infrequently I have mentioned my sisters and brother – Anna, Maria, and Toni. The reason is quite simple, namely that we only very rarely met up with each other. At first, while I was at school as a boarder, we of course only saw each other during the holidays, but then Anna left for her college and then work and marriage, while Maria was at St Andrews, and I was in the Army and after that living in London and then at university. So, there were few opportunities to see each other. Later, Maria would spend Christmas with us. Eventually, Toni lived here and there in London, and then abroad, while I was living miles away in Manchester and Bolton. We were all fully engaged in our own lives.

For the same reason, I rarely saw my nephew Michael until the latter years, other than very occasional visits to Chelsea football matches and rare visits to Anna. This changed when it was clear that Anna was far from well. We then increased our visits to Anna, and she loved us visiting, but it was always fairly clear that she would be unlikely to overcome her medical issues. She clung on and refused to give in, always saying she was 'determined to beat this thing', and reiterated her determination to live till the age of 90. But in the end, she was unable to overcome her problems and passed away in March 2017. I was pleased and privileged to have been asked by Michael and Regine to give the eulogy at her funeral. I had initially declined, as I was not sure if I was up to it. She was the first of the various Pirquet/Pinschof cousins to have died. With our frequent visiting to see Anna, we got to know Regine and Sophie properly.

There had been gaps lasting years of not having sight of Toni, but in recent years, after we moved to Portishead, we have visited him in France on a few occasions. We have thus been able to see how he and Nadine have brought up their three children and how they have matured into very impressive adults. We had been planning to go over in the summer of 2020, but the Coronavirus and lockdown has put paid to that, for this year at least. Maria spent many Christmases with us and otherwise only occasionally, as we rarely travel to London these days, and never since the outbreak of the virus. We last met up during the two London marches, of approximately one million on each occasion, supporting retaining the UK membership of the European Union. Alas, to no effect.

Similarly, I hardly ever saw my cousins, Caroline, Elisabeth, and Antoinette. In the last few years, we have met more often than in the previous 70 or so years! We all met at the wedding of Caroline and David, and then with all their various children and grandchildren at the lovely and rather, or should I say very, unconventional wedding of Sally and Olly. A lovely event.

We then met all our Pirquet cousins again to coincide with the funeral of my cousin John (Pirquet) in Canada, and were able to speak to his family in Victoria, BC. This was a lovely, if sombre day.

We all met – cousins, their children and grandchildren, at our house in Portishead, which was the most centrally situated for all the family.

Margaret and I visited Florette a few times after Franzl died, but she soon moved into an old people's home for her last few years. Austrian standards for the elderly were and are far more advanced and well funded, compared to the UK.

It would be completely remiss of me if I did not mention again the extent to which my Aunt Florette cared for and looked after me in the early years, and provided invaluable help and frequent lodging. At first, when she was living in London, she would always provide a home whenever I was passing or needed assistance that my mother was simply unable to provide, due to distance. When she moved to Reading, she was also there, providing a bed for the night, or many nights during holidays. Without her, life would have been so much more difficult to organise.

A few years ago, we discovered the annual 'Schubertiade' festival held in Schwarzenberg, Voralberg. The festival consists of mainly song and piano recitals, very often by English singers and pianists. Every time we went it made for a lovely holiday, as we drove down and overnighted at some lovely places, especially Nancy. On our first trip to Schwarzenberg, I was persuaded, or I persuaded myself, to do some paragliding! It turned out to be great – at least for me, but not Margaret! We both went up the mountain by the chairlift, and then I went off with the guide who was to take me in a two-seater glider, meaning Margaret had to descend by chairlift on her own. Not the best of our ideas! I believe she was just a little bit frightened when the lift stopped for more than a few minutes (she insists it was at least ten minutes) in order to load up more paragliding enthusiasts for their trip up to the summit. Altogether, it was quite an experience! But perhaps done only once. We went to this festival another three times, and now we both have a longing to return. In fact, when we thought the pandemic was under control, the Schubertiade sent us their brochure for this year's summer concerts. We duly booked, but our understanding of the progress of the pandemic was sadly over-optimistic.

In the summer of 2018, Margaret and I took our car and drove through France, via Burgundy and on down to Avignon, which was lovely. We did quite a lot of driving, such as up to the summit of Mont Ventoux, and were in awe of the hundreds of cyclists, all attempting this famous Tour de France climb and arriving at the top still able to stand. We then visited Orange, and then stayed in Nimes, before returning via central France to a tiny hilltop village and hotel run by an Englishman from Bristol, where he also owned a bar! We then drove to Lac Annecy. Running alongside the lake is a high mountain that one can ascend by car to the summit and achieve a magnificent view of Mont Blanc. Incredible. It must have been 80-odd miles but looked as if it was just around the corner. Lac Annecy and Annecy town itself are just lovely. A compact medieval town with some great food! I would recommend Lac Annecy to anyone.

Again, on the theme of holidays, last year we spent a long weekend in Toulouse. Not a city on the English tourist map, but well worth a visit, as long as you do not go when there is likely to be some civil unrest and some marching, or otherwise called 'organised riots' in the French style. We became caught up in a 'Yellow Vest' march, and were unable to escape the police assault involving the use of tear gas. A Police 'over the top' reaction, again in typical French style. It was not at all pleasant, but some young people who were passing gave us some spray to counteract the gas.

Another holiday last year – the kind of break one only takes in later life (!) – was flying to Vancouver, then taking a two-week cruise on the *Cunard Queen Mary 2* along the inland passageway to Alaska and back, and then going on the Canadian Rocky Mountaineer to Banff, then onto Calgary by coach, before flying back. While in Vancouver, which we were very impressed with, we met my cousin Moni and her husband. They took us on a tour of one of the main Vancouver beauty spots and then to lunch. A lovely day; a lovely couple. A visit to the city and Moni that we would both love to repeat.

Our last holiday abroad was Christmas 2019, shortly before the pandemic lockdown. We all, namely Madeleine and family and Lissie and family, Margaret and I took ourselves off to the Lech, Tyrol, for a week's skiing holiday. Neither Margaret nor I had ever been on a skiing holiday before, though the others had done so frequently. As we were travelling from the airport in Friedrichshafen towards Lech, there was no snow at all, but as we got higher it did begin to snow, and from then to the end of the holiday it snowed most nights to cover the entire valley. The views were stunning. Margaret and I often went up in the gondolas and enjoyed the local food and extortionately expensive shops (without buying). Huge thanks to Marcus for having arranged this holiday, and who made all the bookings and arrangements. We had been hoping to repeat this holiday this coming Christmas, but the virus has put paid to that. Instead, at the time of writing, we have boked to go to St. Anton next Easter – Austrian virus allowing.

As I write, my hobby for the last 20 years, namely pottery, is about to resume after the cancellations following the pandemic. At last I can continue my hobby into my final decline.

Family Photo: Back row from Left: Margaret, Marcus, Rosa, Author.
Front row: Madeleine, Annabelle, Christopher,
William, Elisabeth, Sam.

Grandchildren: Rosa, Annabelle, William, Sam

Family photo Summer 2020: Back row from left:
Christopher, William, Annabelle, Madeleine, Sam, Marcus, Rosa, Elisabeth
Front row: Author Margaret

CHAPTER 14

Recent politics/Dual Citizenship

I cannot end without mention of the dire political problems caused by the Conservative Governments since 2010 in relation to Europe (and many other domestic issues, but I shall desist from commenting on these other policies which would take up too much space, energy, and the need to protect my blood pressure). The sheer stupidity of David Cameron in calling for a referendum on the issue of whether the UK should leave the European Community was astonishing, unnecessary, and a 'cave in' to his far right. These 'far right' clowns were initially a small group of around 12 Members of Parliament who had been against Europe from the days of the then Conservative Prime Minister, Harold Macmillan, in the 1950s. They gave Macmillan, and then Edward Heath, a hard time but both had the capacity, intelligence, and principle to ignore them. The hard right Conservatives had never got over the loss of Empire, and somehow think that the glory days of the Empire (mid-1850's) could be recreated if only we left Europe – plus their own sheer greed, anticipating that they and their business interests would be so much better for themselves when we left. As I have written, the Labour Party was also not immune to this glorification of the Empire, as spelt by the leader of the Labour Party, Hugh Gaitskell. He gave a speech in 1962 saying how outrageous it would be to give up 1000 years of British history. But in the latter case, these sentiments fortunately died out among most Labour politicians after the death of Gaitskell, leaving just a small rump on the left of Labour politics whose concerns were quite different.

To briefly repeat my earlier comments, given the reason for the creation of the European Community – namely to bind Europe together after not only two world wars, but also centuries of warfare between the various European territories – their insight was to understand that reducing the causes of unrest, namely the economy and unemployment, would hopefully do away with the 'competition by combat' for any and all available resources. Or to put it another way, to understand the causes of unrest and to understand its solution is, in the immortal words of President Clinton, 'The economy, stupid'!

Given my family's history as a result of the last war, I was never going to agree to this Conservative European madness. I wrote a longish essay on this issue prior to the referendum, which I sent it to the *Guardian,* who did not publish it. I also sent it to the then deputy leader of the Labour Party, Tom Watson, hoping he would agree and filter it through to his colleagues. He replied that he agreed with most of it. The Labour Party officially campaigned to remain within Europe, but the Labour Leader, Jeremy Corbyn, who would have been part of the Labour far left in the 1960s, appeared incapable of changing his mind from his early days. Though he officially argued during the run-up to the referendum to remain within Europe, his heart was clearly not in it, and it showed. In my opinion, the left wing of the Labour Party is as implicated in the decision to leave Europe as is the lunatic right wing of the Conservative Party. I hope my four grandchildren will study these events and the background to the last war, which can only be fully understood by knowing about the reasons for, and consequences of, the First World War, and so understand recent European history.

What I was appalled at, concerning the issue of the European Union within the UK, was the apparent complete ignorance about the reasons for its creation in the first place. Judging by their public utterances prior to the referendum, hardly any British politician – of any of the political parties – appeared to understand, or give voice to, the basic reasons formulated by the European politicians immediately after the end of the last war. In the UK, only a very few, such as Michael Heseltine, argued for and clearly understood the motivation that led to its creation, as he memorably said at one of the two marches to Parliament Square in the summer of 2019, when an estimated million marched in support of the Union.

(At both of which, Margaret, me, and on the second march my sister Maria, took part.)

A memorable moment was when Jean-Claude Juncker, the then departing President of the European Commission, spoke after his last encounter with the British Prime Minister Theresa May and the final failed attempt to make her see sense. With his head in his hands, and appearing to be on the verge of tears, he said, 'Europe is about peace.' How could Britain and its fanatics campaign to leave Europe, especially after the contribution of Britain in defeating European Nazism? It beggars belief.

The outcome of this fiasco was that I applied for Austrian Citizenship, having been hesitant in my early years, as I have recorded in an earlier chapter. Citizenship was granted, as in fact I had never lost it, apart from 1939-1945 when all Austrians were German! It took two years for my citizenship to be investigated and agreed, and the papers and passport to arrive. Then Madeleine and Elisabeth, Annabelle, William, Sam, and Rosa, also gained Austrian Nationality and Austrian passports. While this may seem academic, it is now possible for all (except for Margaret, Chris, and Marcus!) to travel to Europe without any problems that may or may not follow from the UK's departure from the European Union. In particular, it could be of enormous benefit to any of the four grandchildren who may one day want to study or work in Europe. I DO HOPE YOU WILL REMEMBER TO RENEW YOUR PASSPORTS EVERY 10 YEARS. Austrian bureaucracy being what it is, I could easily predict delays and problems if you were to renew your passports after they had lapsed for some months.

I cannot mention the effort it took to get my passport and nationality certification without crediting the help I received from my cousin Elizabeth. I had to obtain a copy of my parents' marriage certificate before Austria would entertain providing citizenship. The requirements were that applicants for citizenship had to be born 'legitimate'. Hence the need to obtain a parents' marriage certificate. Elisabeth went to the trouble of travelling to the Hirschstetten Parish Priest to arrange this all for me, and I owe her enormous thanks. We did arrange for two bottles of champagne to be sent as a thank you, the least we could do, which I hope she and Christian enjoyed.

As I complete these memoirs, we have been in 'lockdown' as a result of the Coronavirus for a very long time, but restrictions are shortly to be eased – at least until the next lockdown. This has had some advantage, in that I have had more uninterrupted time to write these memories than I would otherwise have had. The weeks have gone incredibly quickly, much quicker than could have been expected. The incredible summer weather of the year 2020 helped, but the absence of seeing our respective families has been difficult. Madeline, Chris, Annabelle, and William have appeared a few times at either our back garden or front door, and we were able to walk over to see Madeleine and family for Annabelle's 18th birthday.

My grandparents would have lived through the last Spanish Flu pandemic, which is estimated to have killed up to 50 million – some estimates say 100 million people worldwide – and to have lasted for three years. So what is the expression? What goes around comes around. We discovered that it is thought by some that the Coronavirus appeared in the Austrian resort of St. Anton shortly after the end of our week's skiing holiday in nearby Lech. We were lucky.

The best we could manage with Lissie and Marcus, Sam and Rosa, was contact via e-mails, WhatsApp, and Zoom. (When I could get the latter working.) It was better than nothing, but not like a proper visit to Cardiff. Margaret and I missed you all very much.

As I write this particular passage, we have just been to Cardiff. Just driving over the Severn Bridge leads to an unexplainable feeling of something that felt like release, but release from what is more difficult to define. Elisabeth said she had the same sense of 'something' when she came over to us in the opposite direction, and again as she crossed the Severn Bridge.

This virus also meant cancelling the Pirquet family meeting in Liege. I do regret the opportunity to meet up again with our cousins and the ever-growing number of their offspring, after what seems a very long time since we all last met. It would be so good for Annabelle, William, Sam, and Rosa to get to know their many cousins.

In response to this new pandemic, the British Government did nothing for ages, almost certainly for ideological reasons and pandering to the far-right wing of the Conservative Party, and their business and banking interests. And perhaps through sheer stupidity and many more absurdities. More to the point is our Prime Minister, who is despised by many as lazy, unprincipled, a liar, and chancer (even by many of his own Conservative Members of Parliament), but is popular with too many of the public so they go along with him. This has resulted in horrendous problems and unnecessary deaths, so if you find that eventually either of your parents and/or grandparents succumb, blame Boris Johnston and this appalling government. Just give us a nice send-off! If it gets us, then fortunately I will have finished these memoirs in time. But both Margaret and I have had both the virus injections, so we should survive.

After the end of the first lockdown, when we all thought the pandemic was at an end, we booked a holiday to attend a Schubertiade, a series of concerts in Schwarzenberg, Voralberg, but as I write now (in May 2001) it has been cancelled. Driving through Northern France, Germany, and Austria, and having to visit autobahn cafés would in any case have been just too risky. Seeing the daily infection rates and deaths in Austria is also enough to say no to this holiday.

An additional but significant problem we have also had to face since October 2020 is a very serious illness suffered by Margaret. She is somewhat better now (June 2021), but by no means fully recovered, and she is due for an operation sometime in this millennium. Pandemic allowing. But I am sure that her illness alone would have led us to cancel Schwarzenberg.

Just as I complete these memoirs, we have news that Madeleine has been made an 'Associate" at her legal firm of solicitors. Great news. Congratulations from Margaret and me.

In the few years I have left, I can confidently look back on my life with no complaints or criticisms. I feel I made the most of whatever abilities I was born with. I had what at times was an eventful professional life, but could not have done anything very much without the constant behind-the-scenes support from Margaret. But above all, I have observed the successful lives of my daughters, their husbands, and their success with their respective children. I am confident that Annabelle, William, Sam, and Rosa will make the most of their contrasting abilities and be successful – politics allowing.

I know they will all look after Margaret if I should depart first. I know they will look after me if I outlast Margaret.

Margaret and I have done our best as parents and grandparents.

A second letter to my grandchildren

I think it appropriate to make some final remarks and comments about my mother, on her decision to join the Benedictine Community of nuns at Minster Abbey, Isle of Thanet, Kent.

I believe it is important for you all to know the full circumstances of her life that led to her decision, and I particularly want to correct the record for those relatives who perhaps did not understand this decision and who quietly – or perhaps more to the point, silently – criticized it. If you all know about her life and the circumstances that lay behind her decision, you will be in a better position to reply to any critical comments.

If one reads my mother's own memoirs of her life once she and her family came to England in 1939 – after just over 11 years of marriage – you may be astonished at the many traumas, difficulties, and long periods of separation from her husband that she had to endure. Following her departure from Austria in 1939, she only had another three years without any separation before my father died in 1949. Only with that knowledge can anyone claim the luxury of criticising. While I can recall some of this period, I only ever knew a very small part of what she had to endure until I read her own account of her life. So again, only an understanding of her entire life in England and the year in the Isle of Man would entitle any relative to make any critical comment.

My mother had had the normal upbringing and schooling for girls within the society and culture that she came from, which concentrated on the boys, and expected girls to be good housewives and prolific breeders. Thus, few had more than a basic education. So when her husband died, she was left with no professional skills. She undertook correspondence courses in domestic science, which enabled her to become an excellent cook/housekeeper. However, after many unsatisfactory periods of employment after the death of my father, my mother moved to Minster Abbey, as mentioned above, initially as housekeeper for the Abbey Guesthouse. My mother loved her position there and seemed to settle in immediately. A major reason was that she got on extremely well with the Mother Superior, who came from a similar German background to her. I suspect my mother was the one person the Mother Superior could really relate to. However, after her frequent moves since my father died, my mother clearly found peace. After a few years looking after the guesthouse, she decided to enter the convent as a nun.

I always suspected that some relatives appeared to be shocked, in particular because they felt that this meant she was neglecting my brother Toni. Toni had always lived with my mother during school holidays, having spent school terms first at Alton School, which he has said was an awful experience, and at a Benedictine boarding school in Herefordshire. I have spoken to Toni about this period, and in particular asked him if he did ever feel neglected by our mother. He said he never felt neglected or abandoned, but if you get the chance, you can ask him yourself how he felt.

In reality, the new arrangement made little if any difference to Toni, who was always made extremely welcome at the Abbey during his holidays. After my mother had entered as a nun, he was able to come down just as before. The only difference was that my mother swapped her room in the guesthouse for one in the main building, and changed her civilian clothes for a nun's habit. But Toni was then accommodated in a room next door to her. My mother carried on looking after the guesthouse exactly as before, which involved all the cooking and cleaning, and so was in and about the guesthouse exactly as before, both during the daytime and evenings. Her frequent attendance in the chapel was just as before.

I mention all this, as inevitably there were members of the extended family in Austria, and perhaps elsewhere, who could not understand her decision, and in particular were critical of what they characterized as her abandonment of Toni. This criticism went on well into the following years whenever I got talking to cousins. It was muted and often understated, or was evident not in what was said, but in what was not said and never mentioned. But nevertheless it was there. She did not abandon Toni. He was not abandoned.

I feel it is important that my family, and all the grandchildren in particular, know her history, so that you can all fully understand and appreciate how difficult her life had been from the outbreak of war and the tragedy of losing her husband so soon after settling down with him and us children in Purley. Should you get either a hint of, or even a mouthful of this criticism from your cousins or others, please do not take any notice. Still better, inform them of the life she experienced after leaving Austria. Her critics were not around then, and will not have known. She deserved a happy life after all her traumas, and she managed to achieve a very happy and a very fulfilled life at Minster. She deserved no less.

Sister Domneva, Authors mother.

www.ingramcontent.com/pod-product-compliance
Lightning Source LLC
Chambersburg PA
CBHW041014140426
R18136800001B/R181368PG42813CBX00028B/1/J

* 9 7 8 1 8 3 9 7 5 8 1 8 8 *